Emotional Child Abuse

Joel Covitz

EMOTIONAL CHILD ABUSE:
The Family Curse

Sigo Press

Boston

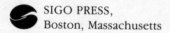 SIGO PRESS,
Boston, Massachusetts

Publisher and General Editor, Sisa Sternback-Scott
  Associate Editors: Becky Goodman
                            Antonia Fried
                            Karen Halverson

Library of Congress Cataloging-in-Publication Data

Covitz, Joel, 1943–
  Emotional child abuse.

  Bibliography: p.
  1. Parenting—Psychological aspects. 2. Child rearing. 3 Child abuse. I. Title.
HQ755.85.C69   1986   649'.1   85–26050
ISBN 0-938434-22-5
ISBN 0-938434-23-3 (pbk.)

Contents

ABUSIVE STYLES OF PARENTING

FROM GENERATION UNTO GENERATION:
REPEATING THE FAMILY CURSE

BREAKING THE CHAIN

There are many people who have made this book a reality. I wish to thank all of them: my patients and friends whose lives I have had the privilege of sharing; my editor, Jane Taylor, who helped make the writing of this book possible; my publisher, whose energy and staff have contributed to the final product; and most important, my wife and children without whose living models this book could not have been written. Some things can only be learned in a family.

Preface

When we look behind the unhealthy narcissistic, egotistical, "me-first" behavior of the adult, we almost always find this root: as a child, this person's *healthy* narcissistic needs were not met. The frustration a child feels when he is not supported, followed, loved and respected can manifest itself in a whole variety of disorders—and when the child grows up, the devastating effects of these disturbances are passed on to his own children. This unfortunate cycle is perpetuated through the generations. I call it "the family curse."

We can break this destructive chain of narcissistic disorders if we first take a close look at the art of parenting. Patterns of abuse will not be altered until parents realize more fully the effect their actions have on their children. When a parent fails to understand the roots and the consequences of the inadequacies in his own development, he will inevitably abuse his children in some fashion. In the chapters that follow I examine the causes and effects of these abuses: parents who are promiscuous, tyrannical, incestuous, smothering, abandoning, overprotective, underprotective, overly critical, jealous, immature; parents who can only love their children conditionally; parents who set unhealthy examples with regard to money, sex, discipline, death; parents who are unable to celebrate their children's lives.

In what I call the democratic family system, the goal is the optimal development of *each* member within the system. The needs of all members are considered of equal significance. Alas, this is not the case with most families. In *The Child in the Family*, Maria Montessori writes, "The child as a separate entity, with different needs to satisfy in order to attain the highest ends of life, has never

xi

been taken into consideration" (p. 15). Psychological child abuse often occurs because there is a lack of equality and respect for the "genuine self," the "authentic feelings" of some family member—especially the children.

Most dysfunctional parenting is unintentional. Psychological child abuse is frequently the result of a combination of the inadequate personality development of the parents (who themselves have not had adequate role models) and the damaging effects of a culture that has abandoned much of its former respect for parenthood. Parents may be the victims of their own parents' failures; they may also simply be unaware of the destructive consequences of their actions.

The psychologically abused child is not a child who has suffered one or two traumatic exchanges with a parent. Children are capable of impressive flexibility when family situations occasionally get out of hand. The episodes and examples in this book were chosen to represent abusive *styles* of parenting, the chronically negative parent-child interactions that severely limit a child's capacity for healthy development.

It is naive, of course, to think that parents, simply by recognizing abusive patterns, can bring up children who are completely healthy emotionally. Parents are human and they are naturally going to make mistakes; parenting is an art, and its practice requires constant refinement and evaluation. But recognition—by parents and children alike—of the roots of narcissistic disturbances is the first step toward ameliorating their effects.

I believe in child-centered parenting. Parents have a responsibility to assist their children in—and celebrate—their positive growth and development, and the fulfillment of their true potential. They must actively recognize their children's needs and work to meet those needs, to nourish their children psychologically. And because the parents' own growth and development are inextricably linked to the growth and development of their children, parents who come to respect, understand and heed their children will nearly always gain a deeper self-understanding as well.

Joel Covitz
Boston, 1985

The Roots of Narcissism

Narcissism: The Disturbance of Our Time

Each age seems to have its characteristic disturbances. Freud found hysteria a prominent complaint; today's therapist is more likely to see patients who are depressed or compulsive, who feel that their lives lack affection, attention and fulfilling relationships.

When we examine the roots of narcissistic disturbances, it becomes clear that most of them are connected to childhood. Simply stated, a child whose early, healthy narcissistic needs (for attention, affection and respect, as well as for food and shelter) are not met has trouble developing strength, independence and self-esteem. Parents who repeatedly fail to meet these early needs are abusing their children psychologically and emotionally. In almost every case, this is the opposite of what the parents intend; they want to be nurturing and helpful, but it doesn't work out that way. In some cases, they simply don't know how to go about parenting. In others, the parents are so needy themselves— because their early narcissistic needs weren't met—that they cannot meet their child's needs. Until these parents can break this chain of abuse, the effect on their children will be devastating and this destructive pattern will likely be repeated in future generations.

The incidence of physical child abuse in our society raises serious questions about the culture in which we live. Battered children who arrive in hospital emergency rooms bearing the

3

wounds of their parents' anger and frustration will carry those scars for years. But children who are emotionally and psychologically abused also carry scars—harder to see at first, but no less crippling and difficult to heal.

One reason, of course, that the problem is so difficult to solve is that these children are generally unable to fight back in any effective way. As Maria Montessori points out in *The Child in the Family*, "No social problem is as universal as the oppression of the child. . . . No slave was ever so much the property of his master as the child is of the parent. Never were the rights of man so disregarded as in the case of the child" (pp. 14–15). Our society regards children as the parents' property. Parents have tremendous power, and children have few effective means of protest against abuse while they are still young. But eventually the price of that abuse will be exacted on the next generation. In her book *Prisoners of Childhood*, Alice Miller writes, " . . . in twenty years' time these children will be adults who will have to pay it all back to their own children" (p. 69).

When a child's narcissistic needs are frustrated, he will usually manifest this frustration in anger toward the parents or in depression. But as the child grows older and gets more "socialized," he tends to repress the anger and tries to behave in a manner that will win or keep his parents' affection (sometimes an impossible task). The repressed rage and hurt must ultimately come out in some form, whether it be a failure to thrive, a poor self-image, self-destructive tendencies, or an adoption of the same mechanisms of defense used by the parents: tyranny, promiscuity, inadequacy. Whatever the adaptive behavior, the underlying frustration does not go away by itself. Only when a child can dig through his own defenses and get to the roots of the problem can he come to terms with his parents' abusive behavior. Almost always, shadows of that parental behavior can be recognized in his own. It is impossible to break the family's chain of abuse completely, to cut oneself off entirely from one's emotional heritage (in its good or bad aspect). But an understanding of the basis for that abusive behavior can help parents and children alike to modify it—with the goal being a step forward for each generation.

There are no secrets from a child's unconscious, although parents sometimes act as though their conscious words and deeds are the only messages they transmit to their children. Much of parents' communication with their children is nonverbal. Subliminally transferred from parent to child, all of the messages will be perceived by the child's unconscious, and he or she will have a fairly accurate perception of the parent's personality. As Jung says in *The Development of Personality,*

> Children are so deeply involved in the psychological attitude of their parents that it is no wonder that most of the disturbances in childhood can be traced back to a disturbed psychic atmosphere in the home. . . . There can be no doubt that it is of the utmost value for parents to view their children's symptoms in the light of their own problems and conflicts. It is their duty as parents to do so. Their responsibility in this respect carries with it the obligation to do everything in their power not to lead a life that could harm the children. Generally far too little stress is laid upon how important the conduct of the parents is for the child, because it is not always words that count, but deeds. Parents should always be conscious of the fact that they themselves are the principal cause of neurosis in their children. (*Collected Works,** Vol. 17, pp. 40–41)

But it must be remembered that the parents alone are not responsible for the family curse. As Jung also wrote, "It is not so much the parents as their ancestors—the grandparents and great-grandparents—who are the true progenitors" (ibid., p. 44).

A child can be set up to repeat a parent's inadequacies. For example, Katherine's† mother had always considered herself intelligent but not beautiful. Instead of trying to deal with this situation, however, she transmitted to her children the idea that only intelligence was important—not attractiveness or social ease or friendships. Her sons and daughter grew up intellectually accomplished but socially inept. Katherine was taught not to value

---

*Hereafter referred to as *CW*.
†Names of individuals referred to in case studies are fictitious, and circumstances have frequently been changed to further protect the individuals' anonymity.

her clothes or appearance. She was always clean, but she described herself as the kind of child whose kneesocks were always falling down, whose hair was out of place. All of her clothes were handed down from her cousins. Makeup was scorned in the household. The children grew up thinking that they were intelligent but ugly, which was not actually the case. Katherine in particular had trouble adjusting socially. She was a victim of the family curse.

As will be discussed later, breaking free completely from one's family curse is almost impossible. But parents *can* become aware of the manifestations of this curse in their children, and can work to change the conditions that foster it. They have an opportunity to change whatever they are able to change in order to make their children's lives more healthy. And as Jung says, "Nature has no use for the plea that one 'did not know' " (ibid.).

Examples of the functioning of today's families given in this book point out some dysfunctional elements of parenting in our culture. Awareness of these deviant behavioral patterns will, I hope, lead to a reevaluation of the needs of family members.

The Roots of the Problem

How can so much go so wrong so early in a child's life? The basic reasons are twofold: the inadequate personality development of the parents, who nearly always suffered abuse themselves as children, and the frustration parents feel, trying to bring up children in a culture that undervalues parenting.

We explore parents' personality development later, but let us begin with a look at our culture. Our children are victims of the increasingly prevalent view that parenting is a messy, frustrating job that gets in the way of one's growth and life, rather than enriching it. The lack of a creative, functioning culture of child-rearing becomes more grievous when we observe the breakdown in family life today. Children of divorce, of abandonment; children, some under ten years old, who run away from home to live in the streets rather than face abusive parents; children who vehemently resolve never to have children of their own; children who become parents while they are still teenagers; children who hate themselves and lash out at others—all are victims, not only of abusive parents, but of a culture that has devalued the art of parenting.

To ask a young woman who is raising two toddlers "But what are you *doing* with your life?" is to tell this mother that what she is doing—the job of parenting—is not worthy of respect. When a culture removes status from the role of mother or father, the self-esteem from assuming that role is lessened. It is as if society is punishing parents rather than respecting them for tackling a tremendously important task. Only jobs in the "real world" seem to earn such respect. One young woman, whose situation reflects that of thousands, decided to go back to work when her child was two months old, even though the cost of day care and other expenses cut into her salary so much that she actually netted less than a dollar an hour. When asked the reason for her choice, she replied, "I don't want my self-esteem to come from my husband telling me I prepared a good dinner for the family."

The desire for self-esteem, and indeed the desire to be a working parent, is not a negative one at all. But it is unfortunate that our culture no longer encourages people to feel self-esteem for the work involved in raising a family. John Bowlby expresses a more encouraging approach with regard to parenting:

> A child needs to feel he is an object of pleasure and pride to his mother; a mother needs to feel an expansion of her own personality in the personality of her child: each needs to feel closely identified with the other. The mothering of a child is not something which can be arranged by rote; it is a live human relationship which alters the characters of both partners.
>
> . . . Continuity is necessary for the growth of a mother. Just as a baby needs to feel that he belongs to his mother, a mother needs to feel that she belongs to her child, and it is only when she has the satisfaction of this feeling that it is easy for her to devote herself to him. The provision of constant attention . . . is possible only for a woman who derives profound satisfaction from seeing her child grow from

babyhood, through the many phases of childhood, to
become an independent man or woman, and knows that it
is her care which made this possible. (*Child Care and the
Growth of Love*, pp. 77–78)

But our culture, instead of encouraging *both* parents to develop
this "profound satisfaction," makes parents frustrated with the
demands the child makes for "constant attention."

For this reason, many couples choose not to have children.
They feel that they should have children only if they want them,
and they view child-rearing as an unwanted burden. If this is their
view, then their choice is presumably beneficial both to them and
to their unborn children. But what does this imply about our
culture? And what are the possible reasons for this decision?

The reasons a person decides not to have children are usually
related fairly directly to his or her own childhood experiences.
The primary reason for the rejection of parenting is that children
are being brought up in such negative, dysfunctional households
that they instinctively do not want to recreate such environments
for any future generation. Many of these children have experienced first-hand what it means to have parents who do not want
them. One patient told me she had decided not to have children
because she wouldn't be able to stand it if her children rejected
her the way she had rejected her mother, and the way her mother
had rejected her grandmother.

People who choose not to have children usually have held this
resolve for as long as they can remember. These people found
childhood a disaster for themselves, and they feel no desire to take
part in the continuation of the life cycle. In light of their experiences, they may be making an understandable choice. But the
increasing number of such choices provides a sad commentary
on family life today. In an age of individualism, the choice not to
be a parent is a person's right—but it may also be a tragic error.

Evaluating the Particular Situation

To determine the nature and extent of emotional child abuse,
each family must be examined in light of its own particular situa-

tion. The family as an institution is one thing; the individual family is another. Every element of the parent-child relationship is affected by this specificity. When we look at any family, we are looking at its unique combination of hopes, education, assets and aspirations. The child is aware of and makes allowances for the particular situation in which he is raised. There is a vast difference, for instance, in a rich parent who brings up his child "poor" and a parent who really has no money to offer.

Keith's father, who was a college professor, said to him, "When I was your age, I had to work my way through college. I had to earn the money for all of my schooling, and I expect you to do the same." Keith saw the flaw in his father's reasoning. Because Keith's grandfather had died when Keith's father was six, he was forced to go to work when he was still in his early teens and had grown up in the lower middle class. But by the time Keith was ready for college, his father was part of the upper middle class where parents generally help pay for a child's education. Keith's father functioned as though he were still stuck at a lower socioeconomic level; he refused to be aware of the special needs and expectations of his family. He failed to understand or realize that developing the ability to deal with the family situation as it is—not simply as one experienced it in the past, or as one might like it to be—is an essential part of the art of parenthood.

Development of the Genuine Self

Narcissus, as the Greek myth goes, stared endlessly at his own reflection. He had no desire to develop his genuine self; he was in love with what has been called "the false self," the self that wants to deal only with the beautiful, pleasant, happy side of life. This fixation cut him off from a full range of life experiences and emotional responses such as envy, jealousy, and anger. This reluctance to come to terms with the disturbing side of life is characteristic of the narcissistically disturbed individual. There is a portion of life which is not conscious, but that is hidden and unavailable. This unknown side can be called the shadow, as these unknown qualities, be they good or bad, remain obscure or in the dark.

As Jung points out, "Childhood is not only important because it is the starting point for possible cripplings of instinct, but also because this is the time when, terrifying or encouraging, those far-seeing dreams and images come from the soul of the child, which prepare his whole destiny" ("On Psychical Energy," *CW*, Vol. 8, p. 52).

The parents' responsibility at this time is extensive. The genuine self is a treasure which each of us is in the process of discovering. Abusive behavior on the part of the parents can inhibit the development of the genuine self of the child.

The Art of Parenting

Sir James Spence, in a lecture called "The Purpose of the Family," said that "one of the principal purposes of the family is the preservation of the art of parenthood." And it is indeed an art. To think that a parent can simply "will" a positive relationship with his child is naive. The will must be there, of course, but it has to be backed up by a commitment to fulfill a child's healthy narcissistic needs for development.

A child facing the difficult challenge of growing up needs a number of things from his parents: their backing and support, their love and encouragement, a sense of stability in the family bond, affectionate exchanges with family members, positive role models, and a sense that his parents love life. A child needs to be liked as a person, a unique individual.

The supportive parent serves as a catalyst for his child, helping him to fulfill his potential. Parenting requires being inspirational, celebrational—and not too objective. When a child of average intelligence wants to become a medical doctor, the school counselor, being objective, may discourage the child from pursuing that goal. This advice, however, may not be appropriate for the parent to give. Not getting into a medical school in the United States, for example, does not mean that the child will be unable to get medical training abroad. The parent must be a spinner of fantasies and possibilities for the child. In *Power in the Helping Professions*, Guggenbühl-Craig states, "Parents often indulge, consciously or half-consciously, in fantasies about their children's future . . . very often . . . these fantasies spring from a basically correct view of a child and represent a creative sighting of its latent potential'' (p. 46).

"If I get into the Boston Symphony, will I make as much money as Daddy?'' my young son once asked my wife. We realized that we should encourage the idea that he might some day be in the Symphony. Later, the child will have to face the reality of his chances directly. But it is important to support a child's dreams at the start, as this support functions as a vital energy source, giving the child a form of emotional and motivational fueling as well as some of the psychic energy he may require to open up possibilities for himself. The parents function as facilitators to help the child become what he feels he must be.

Some parental expectations can frustrate and devour. Since the child is strongly influenced by the unconscious of his parents, he will have a tendency to gravitate toward what his parents unconsciously want him to become. For example, if a child finds that he does not want to have children of his own, it is likely that, on some unconscious level at least, his parents either did not want their child to have children, or never wanted children themselves. These parents may view child-rearing as the factor that inhibited their own development. They may regret their decision to have children; the child may be in their eyes a mistake.

Parents also need to be flexible, yielding to influence when appropriate and realizing that the child often knows what is best for him. The parent must be capable of responding to the child's changing needs. The supportive parent knows how to follow the child, rather than always leading him; he lets the child work out his own destiny.

Children suffering from anorexia nervosa, a disease of self-starvation, typically come from a background where their needs appear to be met when in fact they are not. In *The Golden Cage*, Bruch notes that "these children were well cared for physically, materially, and educationally . . . [but] all these good things were bestowed without being specifically geared to the child's own needs or desires'' (p. 40).

The importance of the parents' participation in the development of the child's self-image cannot be overestimated. Parents can, like the parents of anorectic children, nominally do all the right things, but still miss the mark when it comes to their children's healthy growth, by not being warm and supportive. Jung says, "The curriculum is so much necessary raw material, but warmth is the vital element for the growing plant and for the soul of the child" ("The Gifted Child," *CW*, Vol. 17, p. 144).

A child needs to know that his parents are *living*, not just surviving, and not living solely for the sake of being parents. Mothers today are becoming more aware of the need to develop their own interests, whether in a career or in the home. If parents can get excited about their own lives, they will fulfill one of their basic responsibilities to their children.

Jung also said, "Children are educated by what the grown-up *is* and not by what he says." (*CW*, Vol. 9, p. 175), and "A child certainly allows himself to be impressed by the grand talk of his parents. But do they really imagine he is educated by it? Actually it is the parents' lives that educate the child . . . " (*CW*, Vol. 6, p. 404).

Positive Motivation and Celebrational Parenting

The positive parent will provide encouragement, emotional support, financial backing according to his means, and guidelines to facilitate the child's continued growth without making him or her feel inadequate or overburdened. One can motivate a child to play a musical instrument, for example, by providing good quality instruments and making sure the child has proficient teachers with whom to develop a mutual respect. But after that point, the child should not be pushed. The child is in the hands of the teacher, even though it is the parents who pay for the lessons. A parent can, in fairness, say "If you don't practice, you won't be able to keep on taking lessons"—but after that point he should leave the decision up to the child.

The parent concerned with the child's place in society will motivate him by giving him a realistic view of how people succeed in this society: by having "connections," living in the "right" neighborhood, going to the "right" schools, and so on. He will also motivate the child to succeed on his own terms as well as society's, and to learn how to discriminate between society's requirements and its unnecessary pressures.

The supportive parent will celebrate the child's successes and make the child feel accomplished and proud when he has done well. The celebration validates the child's activities. The inadequate parent, on the other hand, may often celebrate, but only in a narcissistic fashion: he may celebrate and brag about his child to others, making the child his narcissistic showpiece, but he will fail to communicate his appreciation to the child. Such parents are merely using their child to bolster their own low self-esteem. They may expect their child to be successful and be glad when he is, but they don't share their happiness with the child. The child's successes are assumed and taken for granted.

A depressed parent is unable to celebrate even his own successes. The adequate, supportive parent will be able to celebrate *with* his child when things go well. This is one of the most effective motivational tools a parent can use. When a parent fails to respond celebrationally to a child's success, he may inhibit that child's growth. In one case, Gail's fifteen-year-old daughter was dancing at a party for the first time, and many people told Gail how wonderful it was that her daughter was having such a good time. But then Gail's mother said, "You see what your daughter is doing? You're going to have a lot of trouble from her." This was a classic example of a noncelebrational response to a celebrational situation.

Celebrations are life-affirming. Even gatherings in recognition of a death have this effect: funerals imply that life goes on. They are recognitions of death as a significant event. The need to celebrate life's big occasions should not be underestimated. One woman I know said to me, "I had parents who never really celebrated anything, be it birthdays, Christmas or the Fourth of July. We of course observed these special days, but always with a lid on. Never do I remember my father joining my sister and me in a game, or my mother laughing uproariously at something ridiculous." Children need to feel *connected* to the joy of living, and they first sense this connection through the example of their parents.

Birthdays are especially important times for celebrations. One daughter was advised never to remind anyone when her birthday was coming up because then they'd feel obligated to give a present. Her mother failed to realize that birthdays mean much more than presents; they should be happy celebrations of the existence of the birthday child.

Parents who themselves find it difficult to celebrate will often find it even more difficult to celebrate the achievements of their children. Debra told her mother that she had just bought a house and happily described it. Instead of warm wishes and congratulations, her mother began criticizing the house, sight unseen. Another one of my patients excitedly called her parents to tell them the wonderful news that she had just been accepted into medical school. Her mother immediately replied, "How are you going to pay for it?"—with not a word of delight or encouragement.

Healthy parents try to validate their children's choices. They will celebrate a child's decision to go to school, rather than only complaining about the expense. Mary wanted to be a dancer, but her choice was not validated by her mother, who would praise her dancing partners but never praise her. Her mother never asked about her jobs or her dreams; she had no interest in following her daughter. And Lynne's father never demonstrated any interest in his daughter's aspirations to be a lawyer: "As long as you have a roof over your head, don't complain." He couldn't celebrate her dreams with her; he was only willing to validate the basic necessities of life. The celebrational parent, on the other hand, will follow his child and give validity to the events in his child's life.

The functional parent is instrumental in motivating a child to fulfill his potential. He serves as a facilitator by spinning fantasies about the child and by allowing the child to spin fantasies about his own destiny. Such parents work with their children to develop realistic expectations and goals. The motivational parent knows how to celebrate a child's successes, and even encourages the child to outgrow him.

Conditional and Unconditional Love

Love is an affectionate bond between two people which requires that they act on their feelings and be responsible toward the loved one. Bruno Bettelheim used the phrase "Love is not enough"—and he was right. Love for one's child, ideally, can imply that one will act in harmony with his narcissistic needs and do everything in one's power to help him achieve his potential. But too often love is linked with a sense of ownership and a conditional commitment.

Everyone has a need for unconditional love from his immediate family. By unconditional love, I mean that a child's family should basically take a subjective view of him. The result for the child is a feeling that "I am worthy, and worthy of being loved." The parent should go "crazy" over the child. The parent is, in effect, saying to his child, "You are special to me. You can do anything you dream of doing. I have total confidence in you, and I will do everything I can to assist you in your fulfillment."

However, when children lack the ability to alter their impulses, their parents must take some remedial action. When a child gets out of control he is usually unconsciously begging for parental authority. There are limits to what is considered permissible behavior in a normal family, just as adults have to meet minimal standards of behavior to remain within their communities. Overindulgence, a lack of healthy discipline, is not a sign of love, as some parents think. Antisocial behavior is anything but cute, whether in puppies or in children. Parents who overindulge their children are hampering their children's future capacity to function well, and are throwing the family system out of balance. All love, in this sense, has an element of the conditional in it—a sense of what guidelines members of the family respect.

Within the boundaries of normal, understandable human error, the child should be given support and love regardless of his choices, styles, and tastes. Unconditional acceptance implies that a child has the right to be a nurse, or a fireman, or a poet—even though there might seemingly be "better" options. Parents need to recognize that children may go through several choices before settling on an occupation; the parents' task is to help the child explore the different options. This takes flexibility, and a realization that there are many acceptable styles of living.

Leon once told me his parents did not want to go to his high school graduation, saying "What honors are you receiving? What scholarships have you won?" Nothing he had achieved was good enough for them. Susan said to me, "Can you imagine what it feels like, having your mother think you're a failure since you're only a teacher?" Her mother brags about her other two children—one is in medical school and the other is a lawyer—but stops when she gets to Susan, which makes Susan feel unworthy and unloved.

Karl, aged twenty, came to realize his parents' love was only conditional when he told them he was bisexual. His father simply couldn't accept this. "That faggot. He's wrecked. How can I love him?" his father asked me. Maybe some hope for Karl and his parents would lie in family therapy, but it would be difficult, given the father's hostile, negative attitude. Until there is some hope for reconciliation, Karl should move out and start his own life. This parent's inflexibility about his son's choices resulted in the dissolution of positive family feeling. The threat of expulsion from the family system is the equivalent of conditional acceptance. A child feels secure only when he senses that his parents will love him even if they disagree with some of the choices he makes.

Many young people who are compulsively attracted to people who do not love them in return come to realize in therapy that their parents only loved them conditionally. As children they had been programmed to develop one-way masochistic relationships. In *The Golden Cage*, Bruch reports the results of conditional love with anorectic patients:

> Most of these girls had experienced childhood as full of anxiety and stress, constantly concerned with being found wanting, not good enough, not living up to expectations, in danger of losing their parents by acting and behaving as if

they were happy. But all the while, these patients have the secret feeling that they are "undeserving," "unworthy" and "ungrateful" ((p. 39). . . . These youngsters appear to have no conviction of their own inner substance and value, and are preoccupied with satisfying the image others have of them. (p. 43)

Bonding

Bonding in a family starts with the establishment of a long-term relationship between the husband and wife, who both assume the responsibility for maintaining that bond. The bond is then extended to the children, who are made to feel that they are a special and important part of their family's system.

Parenting could perhaps be described in a rather simple way: the parents set up a "nest" for the children, which takes the form of not only a home but a long-term relationship. The goal is to prepare the child for his adult life. The parents must serve as role models, and the children will naturally develop many of their parents' attitudes and patterns of behavior.

Bonding is a lifetime commitment. The child needs and expects this security from his family. The supportive parent is able to sustain being a parent for a lifetime. Although the relationship goes through many transformations, it should never reach the point where the child sees the parent as just another adult. The ability to form an affectionate, loving, long-term bond with a child is the primary step in the process of parenting. It forms the vessel in which the relationship is carried. Parents are the child's natural role models; without that special bond, a child is lacking one of the fundamental foundations for creative growth and development. Bonding sustains the needed relationship between parent and child and facilitates the healthy development of all the family members.

A strong bond between parent and child, especially in the child's early years, is vitally important in the development of the child's ability to bond with others later on. As Michael Fordham writes in "Individuation in Childhood," "In the early months of an infant's life it is essential for him to obtain sufficient good and satisfying experiences of fusion, so that there may be a foundation for later separation. . . . But all the same nobody every truly separates from his or her mother and this continuation of union makes possible recurring and fruitful states of fusion with others in later life" (p. 57).

Bonding gives children a high priority rating on parents' time, energy and assets. It sometimes happens that people who are kind and generous to those outside the family find they have little desire to pay the same respect to their children. Jung said that if a person meets a saint in the street, he should verify the man's sanctity with the saint's wife and children.

Poor or weak bonding can lead to abortive and premature launching. Thomas's bonding with his parents did not last; there was no primary loyalty between parent and child. He was brought up by his maternal grandfather, and his parents encouraged this crossing of generational lines. When his parents came to his town, they would visit his cousins but did not stop by to see Thomas. They gave presents to Thomas's daughter but not to his son, perpetuating the family curse, which was to neglect the sons and favor the daughters. His parents were confused in their priorities: they might have done better to understand that their commitment to their child needed to come before their commitments to other extended family members.

Bondage, as opposed to bonding, occurs when the bond is too tight. It does not permit the child to develop into an independent being but instead makes the child merely the chattel of the parent. Bondage, especially as practiced by older sick parents, or parents with just one child, can be manifested in such statements as "I expect you never to move away from me," or "I need you to visit me weekly as long as I live." Healthy bonding within the family does not require such rules and limitations, since the bond itself is flexible and changes as the family members grow and develop.

The Child Knows Best

The wisdom that children often display is usually related to their intuitive understanding of the workings of unconscious relationships. Many families act on the assumption that adults know best, but children may often have a better perception of their own needs than parents do. In a nursery feeding study it was found that babies allowed the choice of a wide range of foods—some healthy, some not—instinctively chose a fairly diverse, balanced diet.

One girl complained to me that her mother didn't help her to grow emotionally: "She didn't educate my feelings—she left my *feelings* in diapers." This was an accurate intuitive assessment of the situation.

Sharon had the following dream:

> I am with my family and we are packing to go to Mexico. My mother is packing and takes all my shoes, both the ones that are too low and the ones that are too high. Shoes that I haven't worn since high school.

Sharon felt that this reflected her mother's lack of discrimination; she was not following the child. Without understanding her daughter's needs, she wanted Sharon to take "standpoints" which no longer *fit*, whereas Sharon herself intuitively knew which "shoes" were appropriate for her.

One of my patients defined overprotective parents as "people preventing other people from knowing themselves and knowing or learning what is right for them." Once again, parents of anorectic children provide a good example, because their parents seem to be doing everything "right" and yet they fail—sometimes fatally—because they do not *follow* their child and trust that she knows best. In *The Golden Cage*, Bruch observes that "The child's agreeable compliance conceals the fact that she had been deprived by her parents of the right to live her own life. The parents had taken it for granted that it was their task to make all plans and decisions, to direct the child in every respect" (p. 37).

Parents must have the patience to let their children grow and experiment. Jung said, "Proper recognition and appreciation of normal instincts leads the young person into life and entangles him with fate, thus involving him in life's necessities and the consequent sacrifices and efforts through which his character is developed and his experience is matured" (*CW*, Vol. 8, p. 60).

Parents can easily disrupt this maturing process by failing to follow their children.

A child will sometimes sense a need for religious involvement and instruction, even when the parents do not attend church or practice their faith. When one young woman asked to be driven to church, her mother replied, "It's not that we don't want you to go. You can go as soon as you are able to drive there." The daughter interpreted this paradoxical message to mean that they didn't want her to attend. Even though they were not devout themselves, they should have realized that their child was asking for support in pursuing a spiritual direction the child felt it was necessary to pursue.

Children will sometimes even know what is most appropriate for their parents. Jeff, a father of two, had a tendency to form masochistic friendships and was being plagued with demands from his friend Bill. One day just before Jeff left on an important trip, Bill called to say he had a large, heavy bureau to be moved and could Jeff come over and move it for him? Jeff's son took the telephone message, but decided not to give it to his father. When Jeff found this out and asked why, his son answered, "Do you think I was going to let him bother you just before your trip?"

Jeff came to realize his daughter's masochistic friendship with a manipulative girl reflected his own example. As soon as he terminated a friendship with a very inconsiderate, antisocial and sadistic man who had tried to dominate him for years, his daughter followed suit and ended her own nonproductive relationship.

The child usually does know best, even though he may not always be permitted to act on his intuitions. Parents need to be aware of both their child's intuitions and their own, and follow the children without overindulging them. The overindulged child is not given the chance to accept the consequences of his own actions, since the parents will cover for any mistakes he makes. On the other hand, the stifled child whose intuitions are never respected never gets a chance to grow.

The true intuitions of parent and child correspond surprisingly often in the long run. There may be differences on short-term decisions—what instrument to play, what friends to visit, what bedtime to have, and so forth. But parents should focus their attention on helping their child with long-term decisions. A short-term mistake on the part of the child can be chalked up to experience, which is positive in the long run—whereas, if a parent reacts hysterically to a child's choice in the short term, it may damage their long-term relationship.

Maturation, Growth and Development

Parenting is a lifelong endeavor. One's child is one's child from the child's conception to the parent's death, but relationships in the family change and are transformed as its members change. In a functional family system, changes indicating growth are constantly taking place in all of its members. The developmental, maturational process in a child is a gradual movement toward separation and individuation. This process begins at birth and reaches its peak at the end of adolescence.

Freud explored the developmental environments of children—environments which will either maximize a child's potential for healthy growth, or will set a child on the road to neurosis.

The healthy child begins in a basically dyadic relationship with his mother. For a while, the child knows little about anyone else but "the two of us." Gradually it dawns on him that there are others who relate both to him and to his mother. This development of triadic relationships is crucial. If a mother, for example, is only capable of dyadic relationships, she will never allow her child to develop a bond with anyone else. This jealous guarding of the child's affection can be disastrous. As Jung said, "It is not possible to live too long . . . in the bosom of the family, without endangering one's psychic health. Life calls us forth to independence" (*CW*, Vol. 5, p. 304).

A person unable to deal in triads doesn't want to grow—he only wants to be mirrored, like Narcissus. A desire not to have children can come from this early disturbance. If a child's mother prevents anything but dyadic relationships, the child as an adult may be unable to imagine sharing life with more than one person, and thus not want to have children. The adult who is afraid to marry, or the couple who are able to have no friends besides each other may reflect this narcissistic disturbance. If children are to grow up healthy, parents need to respect their needs to explore, to make their own mistakes, and to develop other relationships (with the other parent, with relatives and friends, and with surrogate mothers and fathers—adults who provide role models for the child).

To understand a child's growth process, parents need to recognize that not every one of a child's acts or statements is final. A daughter who goes through a period of lesbianism is not necessarily making a permanent choice. Choosing certain careers, taking a year off from college, adopting distinctive styles of hair and dress, making certain political choices, using drugs such as marijuana, alcohol or cigarettes, deciding to do nothing, becoming promiscuous—all of these moves may be explored by children without becoming permanent lifestyles. They may just be experimental stages or phases in the child's development. A parent who pounces on a child in one of these phases and calls him or her a "faggot," "pothead," "whore," "vagrant," or "criminal" is not sensitive to what the child may need to be exploring.

Children often say, "If only my parents knew what I was doing, they'd go crazy." The child realizes that he must explore different possibilities in his life. The nurturing parent will say, "It may not be something I like to look at, but it may be something my child has to do." The parent must be capable of staying with the child and not prematurely rejecting or labeling him.

The goal of parenting is to promote the optimal growth of the child. In *The Art of Loving*, Erich Fromm writes, "The most fundamental kind of love, which underlies all types of love is . . . the sense of responsibility, care, respect, knowledge of any other human being, the wish to further his life" (p. 47).

Parents can be helpful in guiding—but not pushing—a child toward what the child was meant to be. Their intervention should be evaluated primarily from the long-term result. Forcing an infant or toddler to eat may result in his finishing the supper that evening, but the long-term result may be that the child becomes a finicky eater for the rest of his life.

The toys children choose also have long-term implications. The child who asks for a doll, whether a baby-doll, an anatomically correct doll, or toy soldiers, is manifesting his need for play material to work out some fantasy. Some children may instinctively request a stuffed animal to hold and hug in order to meet a need for physical contact. Puppets are often a good means of meeting a child's need to try out his roles. Good play materials aid the child in his maturation. The parent who understands the importance of play will supply the necessary toys for his children just as he supplies food to meet the child's nutritional requirements. Many television-promoted toys are more related to business than to maturation. The child who asks his parents to purchase something he has seen advertised is often responding to the brainwashing techniques of Madison Avenue. Giving him these inappropriate toys does not contribute to his development and may actually retard it. I once saw a creative toy shop whose logo expressed this notion: "The child who plays well, stays well."

A child's primary sources of information about the world around him are his life experiences, and his fantasy explorations. The parent who deprives a child of these sources of knowledge is abusing that child. Sarah expressed her frustration at her father's unwillingness to allow her to have her own experiences and learn from them: "Anything I did was always wrong. My father always showed me a better way. He was constantly on top of me." The smothering parent is inhibiting the child's capacity for life experience; he wants the child to learn only from the parent's experience.

Some parents treat their children as though they were going to be ten years old forever. "You can get along without sex for three days," says the Puritan father whose unmarried daughter comes home from college for the weekend, bringing the boyfriend she has been living with. But the cruelty in this situation does not lie in the prevention of the young adults' sexual activity. It lies in the failure of the parent to acknowledge the sexuality of the child and the child's need to have a relationship. This failure is abusive because it restricts the development of the child and tries to deny an important part of that child's experience.

A parent who can celebrate his child's healthy growth and maturation will help his child exemplify what Alice Miller in *Prisoners of Childhood* calls "healthy narcissism . . . the ideal case of a person who is genuinely alive, with free access to the true self and his authentic feelings" (p. ix). This parent has the capacity to follow the child's changing developmental needs, and to adapt his behavior accordingly. He has the ability to see the child as a person who is constantly growing and changing, and the parent can grow within his child's life cycle. Jung saw neurosis as a failure to develop. Parents who fail to develop with their children may watch their children being underdeveloped as well, or else they may feel jealous when their children surpass them.

If the maturing process goes relatively smoothly, then ideally the child will separate from his parents and take his own place in the world. Dr. M. Esther Harding wrote:

> After we have freed ourselves from the parents sufficiently to have at least a glimpse of their reality as individuals, we must begin to find a place for ourselves in the world, as separate persons, taking responsibility for our own lives— earning a living, adapting to society, marrying, bearing and rearing children, and assuming our share of the collective burden. (*The Archetypal Images of Father and Mother*, Sec. VI, p. 5)

Or, as Jung put it, " . . . the psychic health of the adult individual, who in childhood was a mere particle revolving in a rotary system, demands that he should himself become the centre of a new system" (*CW*, Vol. 5, p. 414).

The Balanced Family

A family is a group made up of independent but interrelated individuals. The group consists of two basic parts: the individual family members and their interactions. The goal of a democratic family system is the healthy development of all of its members. A sharp line is drawn between the parent-child nucleus and any other relatives and acquaintances. In the dysfunctional family, this primary loyalty is sometimes weak. For example, the father may feel his primary responsibility is not to his wife or children, but to his mother.

People often feel a tension between two roles: as parents, their responsibility is to prepare their children for life; as children, their responsibility is to ease their own parents' pain of old age and death. The danger is that, in attending to the second responsibility, parents will neglect their primary responsibility to their children.

For the family system to function, generation lines must be maintained. In today's balanced family, the primary alliances should be between parents and their children, with grandparents acting as an additional support system. Grandparents can be treated as equal members of the family system so long as their needs do not dominate. The parents' responsibility is to insure the development of their children.

Paul misplaced his family affections in just this way. Paul's father died when Paul was five years old. His mother then left him with his paternal grandparents, and had almost no contact with him. She went to live with her own parents in another country, and she never remarried. Years later, when Paul had married and opened a business, he wrote and asked his mother to come and help by taking care of his children while he and his wife worked, but his mother refused, saying she didn't like to watch children. However, after Paul became successful, he received a letter from his mother requesting that she be allowed to stay with Paul and his family (they now had a babysitter and a cook). Paul and his wife permitted her to come live with them. When she came, she proceeded to interfere time and again with family matters. Because he continuously put his mother's selfish wishes first, he failed his primary responsibility to his wife and children, and he placed great stress on his primary family system.

The primary alliances in a family system should be between parents and their children. If grandparents intrude and try to form a coalition with the children against the parents, they are upsetting the balance of the family system, just as it upsets a business system if an employee runs to the president of the company with every problem instead of to his own supervisor. One parent can also form a coalition with a child against the other parent.

Val's mother formed this kind of destructive allegiance with her daughter against Val's father, who was considered incompetent by both of them. The mutual respect in the family was permanently damaged by this, and Val was never permitted to establish a positive relationship with her father.

In any other enterprise, when a system is created and there is a problem within that system, the originator must assume some responsibility for the problem. Families are lifelong systems in which the parents do just about everything in the early stages. They are truly responsible for the well-being and proper functioning of the family. Later, the children contribute more and more to the system.

In the democratic family system, all share certain basic rights. People are different, and their individuality must be treated with respect. Each member of the system has the right to express himself in words and actions, to ask for what he needs and to offer criticism, and to say what is on his mind to those he knows will listen. Parents shouldn't insist on total conformity to their opinions; open disagreements and discussions should be allowed, based on the understanding that everyone must learn how to cooperate and compromise at times.

Also, in the democratic family system, the parent assumes responsibility for the child for the first thirty years or so. Parents serve as role models; they provide a blueprint for the child's development while also providing love. But affectionate exchanges go both ways within the family system. The child who is the recipient of parental affection, concern, and love will normally develop a loving, affectionate bond with his parents.

In the family system, the parent grows through the process of parenting. Different parts of the parents' personalities are touched at different stages of the child's development, and many things required of one as a parent will force one to mature as a person. When people have children, they need to learn to balance their roles as individuals, mates, and parents. Flexibility and maturity are important in handling the necessary compromises of family life.

Running away from being a parent is often running away from one's own development; it can be a childish form of narcissism. Some parents seem only able to deal with babies; they are too immature for the later stages of parenting. There are also parents who hate babies, but what they may be communicating is that they cannot deal with the infantile side of their own personalities. The desire to offer love and help and the willingness to compromise that are essential to parenting are life-enriching habits. People who choose not to have children may be missing important developmental benefits that child-raising could bring them.

One woman I know felt ambivalent about having children because she was successful in her career. When she was thirty-five, she and her husband decided to have children, but she expected to feel that she had sacrificed her career for them. She was surprised when she realized that she was happy to give up her career for her child—or, in her own words, "I didn't realize what would happen when I fell in love with the child."

Setting the Stage for Narcissistic Disorders

Significant choices that will help determine how a family will function and the environment in which the child will grow should be made by couples even before they are married. When decisions about marriage, childbearing and attitudes about raising children are made casually and narcissistically, with regard only for the couple's immediate needs, the children will suffer.

Marrying the Wrong Mate

Many parents set up a nonfunctional environment for their children long before the birth of those children by failing to realize the importance of the marriage axis on which the family revolves. Although differences can be invigorating when there is mutual respect, in some marriages it is clear from the outset that the possibility of establishing a satisfying, long-lasting bond is improbable. Difficulties often arise when parents come from drastically different educational and social backgrounds, or when they marry simply because they are getting older and fear they won't find anyone else who will have them. The chemistry between the parents is one factor that determines the kind of parenting that will take place.

A woman may marry a man she thinks is a "loser," but console herself with the thought that at least he will give her children. Her feelings cannot fail to be transmitted to her children, who are

29

probably predestined to see their mother as a plotter, and their father as a failure.

Annemarie, for example, realized that her parents were unable to interact as equals; one was always looking down on the other. Her mother scorned Annemarie's father for his problems with alcohol and his inability to do anything but earn money and to fix things around the house. He was a handyman, but not a man. Annemarie recognized that her father was weak and that her parents were mismatched. Her father's symbolic place in the household was crystallized for Annemarie in a dream image in which she saw him as "junk on the lawn."

Any marriage in which one partner has low self-esteem is likely to be unstable since that partner will look to the other as a problem solver, and then, paradoxically, feel threatened by the differences between them.

Children will invest as much energy as is needed to ensure the preservation of family harmony, even if it means sacrificing themselves to do so by developing psychological disorders. The emotionally abused child usually exhibits symptoms which make it appear that he is sick, but which may actually be distress signals about his parents' marriage. He knows that his own growth is being inhibited by his parents' pain and tries to absorb that pain for them. As for the parents, if they focus their attention on their "problem child" rather than on their own marriage, a burden is lifted from them, and they come to have a stake in the preservation of their child's sickness. Instinctively, the child may be trying to unite his parents by getting them to pay attention to him. "I'd rather be sick," he seems to be saying, "if being sick means you two will work together to make me better." This makes intuitive sense, because the child fears that if his parents' marriage breaks down utterly, he will be left out in the cold.

Marrying for money is also a destructive practice which can have unfortunate effects on the children. In the past, this has seemed especially true when a poor or middle-class man married into an upper-class family. A person who marries for money is always aware, on some level, of the precariousness of the situation; the power lies in the hands of the wealthy partner and for the unwealthy spouse one false move may mean a return to a poorer mode of living. One father who married for money had a recurring dream that he was the caretaker of his wife's estate. Children sense this imbalance and the resulting uncertainty in the marriage, and it can deprive them of the stability they need from their parents. In an unequal marriage, children cannot assume, as they ought to be able to, that the bond between their parents is solid.

"Planned" Parenthood

Whether consciously or unconsciously, parents plan to have the babies they have. Parents may claim that a pregnancy was an accident, but in most cases, parents *plan* to have an "unplanned" baby. "Planned parenthood" implies that some families happen accidentally. But from a psychological point of view, in which unconscious wishes are considered as valid as conscious ones, accidents are extremely rare. What seems to happen in most cases of "unwanted" pregnancies is that the pregnancy was wanted, but not the responsibilities of following through, of having and raising the child.

When we choose our life styles, we are ethically responsible for the consequences of those choices. But the consequences of pregnancy are enormous, and it is tempting for parents to shirk them. These attitudes could lead to abuse.

Not everyone is cut out for parenthood, and pressure exerted from outside the family by would-be grandparents or religious doctrines could contribute to a situation where children are set adrift because their parents are not ready or able to assume responsibility for them.

I Never Wanted You

Children can sense when their parents are frustrated and disappointed with them. Annie felt just this way:

> . . . [I] was born a disappointment. By the time my sister was
> six my mother had become concerned with my sister's at-
> tachment to her. She felt that another child would even
> things out and promised my father a son. The story goes that
> he was so angry at the news of my birth that he went to a
> stable and rode for several hours before he was ready to see
> me. His cousin had delivered me, and my father didn't speak
> to him for some time.

A mother who suffers from chronic depression may find it
especially difficult to be celebrational at the birth of her child. A
newborn child will sense a mother's rejection at such a time, and
will probably feel that he is somehow the cause, and that he is not
really wanted.

The unrealistic fantasies parents sometimes have about having
children are often shattered by the reality of demanding newborns
who may not always be sweet, cuddly and cute. "Ideally," say
the Kempes, "a wanted child is regarded as lovable by both
mother and father; they support each other and are delighted with
their roles as parents." But, they go on to say, "some children are,
right at birth, perceived by one parent or the other as simply so
different from prior fantasy that their perfectly normal newborn
behavior, such as soiling and crying, is regarded negatively, and
no bonding of love develops." In the worst cases, "the child is
a disappointment and is let known that he is. Whether he was
'lovable' or not in the first place, he quickly becomes to the
parents a veritable monster, and bonding in hate may result"
(*Child Abuse*, p. 26).

The medical syndrome known as "Failure to Thrive" can result
under these conditions. Children with this condition fall behind
in their normal growth, although there is no apparent physical
neglect. Instead in many instances, emotional deprivation is
thought to be the cause; the child who is unnurtured will, in effect, stop maturing physically. Children whose parents do not
want them and cannot form an affectionate bond with them may
also fail to thrive psychologically.

The Only Child

Some parents have so many children that everyone in the family is overwhelmed, and no one receives adequate attention. But the choice to have only one child can be at least as dangerous, since the child is more than usually prone to become a neurotic, over-protected, pressured individual. The only child is in a hazardous position in the family system; his chances of meeting his narcissistic needs without having the burden of over-great expectations placed on him is slim. The problem stems from overvaluing the only child. All of the parents' fantasies about their offspring are focused on one person. The only child is always in the limelight. The pressure is always on. The fantasies the parents have about the only child are usually a burden to him. When a child receives the unconscious messages "You are all I have," "My only hope lies in you," "I can't wait until we can plan your wedding," "You must give us grandchildren," or "I hope you become a professional," he may feel that he has been programmed to perform in a certain manner just to please his parents, and that he must not disappoint them.

Rollo May puts it this way in *Love and Will*:

> . . . imagine the couples—and, with the need for population control, there will perforce be many—who will plan to have only one baby; consider the tremendous psychic weight this poor infant will have to carry. As we see in our therapy, particularly with professional people who have had their one child, there is a great temptation to overprotect the infant. When he calls, the parents run; when he whimpers, they are abashed; when he is sick, they are guilty; when he doesn't sleep, they look as though they are going to have nervous breakdowns. The infant becomes a little dictator by virtue of the situation he is born into, and couldn't be anything else if he wanted to. And there is, of course, the always complicating and contradictory fact that all this attention actually amounts to a considerable curtailing of the child's freedom, and he must, like a prince born into a royal family, carry a weight for which children were never made. (p. 120)

When this problem is compounded by the loss of one parent, the bond between the child and the remaining parent can become unwholesome. In one case a boy whose father died when the boy was three was brought up by his mother. He was an only child and never had a father to serve as a role model. He and his mother, therefore, were dangerously close, and this got in the way of his other relationships. This situation also became limiting for the mother in that she displayed an inordinate amount of interest in his private conversations with friends; she never dated and had no friends; he was her only relationship, and she lived vicariously through him. If he had had a sibling or two, or if she had gotten involved with another man, this situation would likely not have arisen. It is important for a child's sexual identity that he see a parent as a social and a sexual being, and that he see his parents express their sexuality in appropriate relationships rather than (as often happens with single parent/only child situations) focusing their sexuality on the child.

In the old-fashioned extended family situation, with brothers and sisters, grandparents, aunts and uncles present, there were some checks and balances to guard against poor parenting. But in a one-child family, problems can arise if the child is isolated, with no other input than his mother or father. Only children should be encouraged to search out other role models, and to establish a healthy independence from their parents.

The Promiscuous Parent

Young children are very concerned with the survival of the intimate relationship between their parents; they are, especially when younger, basically conservative and believers in monogamy. If parents choose to experiment with their sexuality, they must take responsibility for the effects of their actions on the family, and realize that their children can be victimized by these actions.

An extreme example of this problem was that of Patricia, who found out about her mother's premarital sexual adventures and that her mother married only to have children, and not for love. She sensed the basic instability in her parents' bond, and this may have contributed to Patricia's instability and to the fact that she had to undergo a series of stays in a mental hospital.

On the other hand, Amy had to deal with her mother's promiscuous style in that she was asked to change father figures as often as her mother changed partners. She had always assumed that her mother's husband was her real father. But because this man had never been sure that he was her father, he had no confidence in fulfilling his role. When Amy discovered this in late adolescence, it became clear why they had such an ambivalent relationship and why for years she had fantasized that he wasn't really her father. Amy's situation was further complicated by her mother's subsequent divorce and remarriage, after which Amy was told to refer to her mother's first husband (her alleged father) as an uncle, and to pretend to her friends and neighbors that her new stepfather was her real father.

A promiscous woman who cannot change her style before she has a child is unfair not only to the father, but to the child. If a man cannot be certain he is the father, the child will pick up on his uncertainty. Even if the mother's husband is consciously presumed to be the father, the child will sense the unconscious doubts in his parents and will suffer.

When a parent is promiscuous, the child will more than likely have a distorted view of sex. The parent may enjoy sex, but not pass on the idea that sex is a complex, emotionally involving activity. In the case of two sisters, for example, it became evident that they both struggled in adulthood with their connection to their feminine sexuality. One of these women, a photographer, seemed compulsively attracted to women's genitals, photographing them often. Her sister was a lesbian. They later found out that their father had been highly promiscuous during his marriage. He and his wife had secretly agreed to postpone divorce "for the sake of the children" until after the sisters were grown. Their parents' unsatisfactory relationship, in which love and sex seemed unrelated, left the sisters with an inability to relate the two. They were trying to connect with female sexuality in some way, through photography or through lesbianism, because their father's promiscuity and their mother's tacit acceptance of it had distorted their ideas about relationships and sex.

The Self-Centered Parent

Self-centered parents see themselves as the focal points of their families. The father is king of the hill, the mother queen of the palace. These parents define their own narcissistic needs as primary and the need of other family members as secondary. They do not respect the "we" of their family, showing primary concern for the "me," and so set up problems for their children, whose age-appropriate narcissistic needs will not be met. The self-centered parent is expressing the erroneous notion "I gave you life, and that is enough" or "I gave you life." And the emphasis is on the "I" as if childbearing was experienced only by the parent.

We live in an age of selfishness, one in which many parents expect as a matter of course to meet their own needs first. One boy's father told him, "After me, you come first." Parents' narcissistic needs often conflict with the needs of children, but particularly when children are young, parents need to be flexible. In a *Wall Street Journal* article, Edward Wynne wrote, "A married couple that plans to have children must make a serious commitment to the task—which means it may have to sacrifice other prestigious goals: optimum career advancement, geographic mobility or the option of easy divorce."

When children are older and needs conflict, a compromise is called for—something akin to balancing the family budget. This can become impossible if any one member, especially a parent, has the type of needs that threaten to "break the bank"; the needs of each family member are equally important. If any imbalance does occur, in a compromise the child should be given a slight edge.

Responsibility in the Early Years

The awesome task of helping children develop their potential is very difficult for some parents to accept. The responsibility goes through many transformations as the child grows, and at any point parents can fail to grow with these changes. The implicit refusal to let a child develop into an autonomous individual, different from his parents, can have negative consequences when the child is still quite young. Its effect may be manifested in separation anxiety, when the child does not want to go to nursery school where he will have to survive without his mother and father, or when he is left with a babysitter. Some amount of anxiety in these situations is normal, but certain parents unconsciously encourage it because they also fear the separation.

Parents can display irresponsibility in many ways in the early years when children are particularly impressionable. Naming a child, for example, is sometimes taken lightly by the parents, but it is the child who must suffer the consequences of being named Cuthbert, Iphigenia or Newt. One parent I know named his child Chamor, which is the Hebrew word for donkey. Parents can also be irresponsible in their seemingly idle comments, not realizing how seriously they will be taken by their children.

Children are always observing their parents, and are inevitably influenced by their actions. I once saw a woman in a toy store give her small child a breakable item from a high shelf to play with. The child broke the toy, and the saleswoman informed the mother that she would have to pay for the item. When the mother protested, the saleswoman suggested a compromise and asked that she pay half the cost of the toy. "I refuse to," the mother said, although her own irresponsibility initiated the problem. After refusing to pay, the woman took the child and stalked out of the store.

The opening moves of parenting relate to a person's attitudes about parenting and to the heritage a person brings along when the decision to have a baby is made. Ideally, the parents feel excitement and openness about being parents, and have had positive role models themselves. They have some sense of what lies ahead of them, and a willingness to see the experiment through. If parents have realistic and hopeful expectations about marriage and parenthood, and are able to deal thoughtfully and spontaneously with problems as they arise, they will be able to attend to their children's healthy narcissistic needs and will set the stage for positive development.

Abusive Styles of Parenting

The Inadequate Parent

Parental failure often relates to a failure in personality development. A parent with low self-esteem will feel inadequate, and therefore act inadequate. An unconfident parent will not be able to guide his children with confidence. When a parent needs his child to support his own deficient or weak ego, the child may attempt to meet the needs of his parent, and in so doing may sacrifice the fulfillment of his own narcissistic needs. The parent's personality needs may act like a magnetic force, drawing the child into the role of therapist. The problem is exacerbated by the child's natural identification with his primary love objects. When these love objects have narcissistic needs that were not met, the child may identify with or internalize the parent's fragmented ego and may manifest some sort of separation panic—a fear of entering the world because he feels his resources are not sufficient to cope with it.

The child may attempt to compensate for his parent's personality deficiencies by reacting with solutions—albeit inadequate ones—to the situation in which he has been placed.

On the other hand, a child may have a positive reaction to a negative situation; some children can turn a parent's weakness into a source of motivation. But this kind of reaction usually takes place only when the child's other parent is strong enough to fill the roles of both mother and father, or when a surrogate parent, such as a grandparent, is available.

41

The adjusted child works on solving his own problems in life, whereas the neurotic child may be trying to solve his parents' problems. Family therapists have discovered that children will often sacrifice themselves by developing disturbing symptoms in order to give their parents a focus and to allow their parents to repress their own problems.

Jason came to realize that he was trying to solve his boss's problems at work and his father's troubles at home. Although he was not a management-level worker, he worried greatly about the success of the company for which he worked. His dreams were full of images of himself helping his father, his siblings, his football coach—anyone Jason thought needed assistance. Jason placed his own problems on the back burner while trying to please the people he admired. He once wrote in his diary:

> I lie in my bed . . . wondering about my father, realizing humanness in him. He walks so tall, so strong, yet emotionally people get under his skin. Drinking is a problem for him. I love him—I realize I didn't have to battle him—I can help him get away from his bizarre, draining, tiring life.

Jason's father had never paid the slightest attention to his son except to berate and manipulate him, yet Jason felt the need to help his father grow up!

Sally felt that her mother was emotionally undernourished, and she found herself constantly protecting her and taking care of her. However, when she got older, Sally found that she was tired of mothering her mother—or anyone else. Dreading the thought of having to provide psychological nourishment for another person, she sought relationships in which there was no commitment.

Children of inadequate parents often have to take on parenting roles in relation to their siblings, too. One 28-year-old woman complained that she was sick and tired of playing Mom to her younger brother, lending him money and looking after him. Her own mother was unable to fulfill her proper role and the daughter had to act as a substitute.

The Immature Parent

Some parents never really grow up. Their immaturity prevents them from providing the supportive atmosphere their children need. Parents should be the leaders of their families, but some choose to play a weaker, safer role instead.

In such a case, Arthur was disturbed by the sterility of his home life and the immaturity of his parents. He had a dream reflecting this in which he saw his father's room in a "bleak house." In the dream, his father had brought a woman to his own room and she was seducing him. Arthur realized that part of his problem stemmed from having a father who was too immature to assume responsibility for his own sexuality. His father was able to structure the encounter in such a way that it appeared that the woman was in control. In real life, Arthur's immature father often displayed this kind of promiscuous, compulsive behavior.

Occasionally parents seem to structure their lives so that they never have to become full, responsible adults. Those who follow this pattern may marry, but they are not likely to explore all the potential in their family systems or in their work lives. They may be asocial, refusing to fit in with the group. Children who grow up with such parents may feel that they are living in single homes, rather than in families.

Karla's father was a reclusive alcoholic who functioned well only at work. His role in the family was primarily as the provider of material goods. Emotionally he simply wasn't there. According to Karla, he was always in hiding. Karla's mother had trouble establishing a successful bond with him, and consequently Karla felt that her parents had, in effect, remained single. Their marriage did not display what I call psychological/emotional closure. Physical closure in a marriage implies that it has been sexually consummated. But psychological/emotional closure implies much more: it means that the functional, wholesome marriage (or long-term relationship) has longevity, durability, stability, balance and commitment.

When two people of low self-esteem marry, their bond is likely to be immature. Although it may seem that they're in love with one another, they may simply be obsessed with each other, or clinging to each other because they can't face being alone. They may make excessive demands on each other's time, not allow each other to have outside friends, check up on each other constantly, live in an isolated area, and never really trust one another. All of these immature tendencies indicate the parents' inability to create a satisfying, trusting bond.

Miguel couldn't tolerate living alone, so when he moved away from his wife, he went immediately to live with another woman. Miguel's daughter sensed his immaturity and resented it. When she overheard him talking to a mistress on the telephone and told her mother about it, Miguel was terribly hurt and felt that his daughter must not love him. He didn't understand that by doing this she was identifying with her mother. He complained of his daughter's bratty behavior, unwilling to face the idea that he was the one who was being immature.

Immature parents may display inappropriate and at times outrageous behavior, not understanding how to act in the society in which they live. The parent who dresses inappropriately, who insults the child's friends, who does not keep himself or his home clean, who is loud-mouthed or foul-mouthed or leaves pornography lying about the house, can be an embarrassment for the child. One man I know allowed his girlfriend to take showers with his eleven-year-old son, imposing his own chaotic life style on the child. Children generally want their parents to be normal, like "other people's parents," and they may feel like social misfits themselves, when their parents are not proper role models.

Some inadequate parents go so far as to use their children as pawns in their own relationship. Jim and his wife Barbara quarreled frequently, sometimes about Barbara's alleged promiscuity and Jim's physical abuse of her. When she finally threw Jim out of the house, he told people in the neighborhood that she was a whore, and spread the rumor that one of his two children might well be illegitimate. He did not hesitate to sacrifice the well-being of his children for the sake of revenge.

Another example of the inadequate personality in a parent is the latently homosexual or transvestite father who may outwardly be heterosexual in his orientation, but finds it impossible to form satisfactory long-term relationships with women. He is thus providing an inadequate role model for his children. The example he provides suggests that men and women cannot be happily married. It is also a sign of developmental immaturity for a homosexual to get married and have a token child just as a cover.

The immature parent may seem unable to get his life together. He may find that he has no energy, no drive to go out and do things. He may try to avoid his problems altogether. He may take out his frustrations on his spouse: physical abuse is a manifestation of low self-esteem and immaturity. Or he may spend all of his time compulsively at work or on his hobbies, afraid to be alone with himself or with his family. Curt perceived his own inadequacy and the consequent disturbance in his family in a dream in which he sensed that there was some "anarchy going on" outside him, and that he had to bar the doors to keep the confusion from breaking in. The anarchy represented in the dream was actually manifested in his family. His wife was openly having an affair with another man, and the family had lost its stability. The system was in chaos, and Curt did not know how to bring order back into it. He was not mature enough, he realized, to stabilize his family life. In a situation such as this, each of the parents is acting out his or her inadequacies, and the tragedies perpetrated are not only experienced in the alienated relations of the parents, but in the children unwittingly becoming the victims.

Boost My Ego

The inadequate, immature parent often needs his children to encourage and protect him, to take care of him and boost his ego. In a sound family system, it is the parents who function as fans of their children, and not vice versa. Of course there are times when children will rightly be proud of their parents—but parents must not rely on their children's pride in order to increase their own low self-esteem.

The parent who expects his children to be his fans will prove inadequate because there are times when being a parent does not make a person popular with his children. Parenting is not a popularity contest; there are bound to be points of misunderstanding, and parents must be capable of tolerating the temporary loss of their children's affection that may result. The parent who is not able to do that will inadvertently turn his child into a tyrant, by bending to all of his wishes. Insecure parents with low self-esteem will tend to overinvest in a child, placing a tremendous burden on the child to succeed, and thus vicariously raising their own self-esteem. In *The Golden Cage*, Hilde Bruch said of anorectics: "These children believe they must prove something about their parents, that it is their task to make them feel good, successful, and superior" (p. 25). That should not, of course, be the child's task.

One mother was blatant about her request for an ego boost. She went to visit her daughter Shawn and announced as she came in the door, "I intend to make things hard on you so that you can prove your love for me." She tried to make Shawn feel guilty by claiming that she had stayed married to her abusive husband just for Shawn's sake, and that her working while Shawn was growing up was a monumental sacrifice for her daughter. If Shawn had praised her throughout all of this, she would have felt happy; her own low self-esteem prevented her from feeling good about herself in any other way than through forcing her daughter's affirmation of her.

I often hear children say how proud they are of their parents: "They are finally becoming well-adjusted. They are mellowing out in their old age." But this is usually after the parents have already damaged their children's development. These immature parents have grown up too late.

Take Care of Me

Similar to the parents who demand that their children admire and be proud of them are the parents who are so unsure of themselves that they narcissistically need their children to change their lives and plans in order to protect, please and take care of them. These children are constantly being begged to visit their parents, to write to them or call them weekly, not to abandon them, not to move far away. Similarly, these demands are increased when the parents are senile, sick, or dying, but those problems are somewhat different and will be treated separately.

Jacques expressed his frustration with his mother's inadequacies by saying that his mother was lonely and wanted him to fill her empty hours. Jacques himself liked being alone and private, but when he was alone he was also aware that his mother must be alone, and he was made to feel guilty about it. He felt that her insecurity infringed on his right to be by himself.

The parent with an inadequate personality often cannot keep separate the various roles a parent must play. A mother is an individual, a mother and a wife, and the roles are distinct. The adequate personality is capable of understanding that the destruction of her relationship with her husband should not destroy her child's relationship with his father. Doris' mother inappropriately turned her children into confidantes: "Let me tell you what your father did to me," she would say, and launch into her tale of woe. "Can you imagine how I felt when I found another woman's mark on his underwear?" She felt that since he had betrayed her, he had no right to be a father either. She was trying to elicit sympathy and comfort from her children, denying them their own relationship to their father, and begging them to take care of her.

Frances' father was so insecure that he clung to her very tightly. She felt she knew him thoroughly and was privy to his true emotions. She knew she could not tell him that she didn't want to stay with him, because it would have been one more thing that would make him "heavy and somber." It would be interpreted as a rejection of his fathering. So she felt she had to protect him, since they were "like pals."

Many children have to adjust their lives to their parents' needs this way. In an extreme case, Brett related that when she told her mother she wanted to kill herself, her mother said, "But your father loves you so much. Don't kill *him*." She thought of her daughter's suicidal wish only in terms of her husband's needs.

Similarly, one mother said to her son, "When you're sick, who suffers?" meaning that she suffered more than he did, and so for her sake he should not burden her with his illnesses.

Many children with alcoholic parents are burdened with the request, spoken or not, to "take care of me." Such children are forever having to make excuses for their parents' conduct, get them medical help, and deal with their unhappiness and their rapidly changing moods. The burden on the children is usually not acknowledged by the alcoholic parent, and sometimes the other parent may ignore it as well.

Misrepresentation and Family Misconceptions

The inadequate parent often passes along to his children inaccurate, unhelpful ideas about life, work and relationships, which may harm the child's development.

Sex is consistently misrepresented to children. Many children are given the idea that sex is only acceptable as part of marriage and for the purpose of procreation; the pleasures of a loving, intimate relationship and the pleasures of the body itself are never mentioned. The immature parent may lie to his children about where babies come from, or give them irrelevant, inappropriate advice about relationships—"Women are only after your money"; "Men are only after your body"—which reflects their own inadequacies and fears.

The compulsions of promiscuous parents may give the child an inappropriate attitude toward sex. The parent who fails to offer his child the role model of a responsible adult, but instead behaves like a perpetual adolescent, misrepresents one of life's most significant experiences. Parents whose marriage relationship tolerates an unsatisfying emotional element but continues to function on the physical level teach their children that love and sex aren't connected. This sometimes results in a child who is compulsively active sexually, often to the point of apparent "oversexuality," because he is driven toward sexuality without knowing how to develop a surrounding relationship.

Lee found that she had trouble getting into a mutually satisfying relationship with a man. She came to discover that she had many misconceptions which were undermining her conscious wish for a close connection. She thought it better to have a poor relationship than none and that you could only get into a relationship by completely pleasing the man. As a result, she never showed her genuine self to a person. She was able to trace this misconception back to her father, whose plans for her were extensive and rigid. Her father gave her only conditional acceptance—the condition being that she fulfill his fantasy of her. She learned, to her dismay, that she only felt loved when she wasn't being herself. She became other-directed rather than inner-directed, and found that though she would work hard to please the men in her life, she wasn't a full person within the relationship.

Parents often pass on rules about relationships which, although unsound, are taken as gospel by the whole family. When one young woman was debating the pros and cons of a particular relationship with a man, her mother said, "If you have so many questions, you haven't found the right man." But questions are necessary in the development of healthy relationships. Another mother told her daughter that there was no such thing as a platonic relationship. This notion—that every friendship she had with a boy had to be charged with sexuality—distorted her view of adolescent friendships. Marianne's mother told her, "Don't go looking for boys; you will find a man when you aren't looking for one." This kept Marianne from dating; she sat at home waiting for the right man to come along. And Jack's father told him that if he was tall, handsome, dressed right, and went to good schools, he would be successful. Jack had all of these qualities, but he was still continually depressed; his father had misrepresented to him what really made people happy.

Patrick's father told his son to "always make yourself number one." When Patrick's father put himself in the number one position, he considered the good of the family system less important than his own selfish needs. Parents may reasonably want to impart to their children the notion that they ought to take care of themselves and have a healthy measure of self-respect. But the parent who tries to bolster his inadequate ego by following, and dispensing, the bad advice that one should always think of oneself first is not providing a developmentally sound atmosphere for his child. Patrick found himself cheating his friends and acting selfishly, thinking primarily of his own interests, just as his father had taught him. It was not until years and several unfortunate relationships later that he realized the destructive consequences of his selfishness.

Parents also pass along distorted attitudes about work. Jason was highly successful and needed by his company, but he found that he was often negative and angry on the job, striking out at his boss. Since he was a good worker, his boss tolerated him, but he was not liked. His father's irrational anger had set up this similar pattern in Jason.

In order to change, Jason first had to recognize the destructive pattern he had inherited and identified with. He was so psychologically bound to his father that he was socially stunted. Jason had to focus on his own development for a while, away from his father and his career. He began to redistribute his energies, getting more control over his life by considering his options—moving away from his father, switching companies, even switching professions.

Another woman felt lost, not following her own inclinations but instead following her parents' wishes that she give up music, which she loved, and become a doctor. She was following her mother's pattern, since her mother had given up her own career in order to have children. After much reflection, she realized that she had internalized her mother's misconceptions, which required a child to study for a lucrative, secure profession, giving up ideals as frivolous. She was now in the wrong city, pursuing the wrong goal by studying medicine. She was involved in unsupportive relationships, where her own needs were constantly ignored. If her parents had expressed their nurturing love by allowing her to follow her inclinations and by supporting her in them, she might have been much happier. As it was, she lost respect for her own needs until she gave up medical school, moved to another city, broke off her destructive relationships, and pursued a musical career.

Religion is another common breeding ground for hypocrisy and misrepresentation. Parents who are too strict with a child in matters of religion, allowing the child no free choice and no responsibility for making up his own mind, are potentially setting up sources of extreme conflict for the child as he discovers that society's norms and mores often do not jibe with those of his religion. Religious schools and seminaries are sometimes used as reform schools, to keep children off the streets, and the discipline that should normally be handled by parents can be transferred by the immature parent to the fathers and mothers of the church. Threats of hellfire or damnation, or the burden of excessive guilt for minor misdeeds, can produce extreme reactions in the vivid imaginations of children.

The opposite extreme, in which parents give no thought or attention at all to the child's spiritual development and philosophical questioning, can be just as destructive. When parents are involved with different religions, or when one parent is devout and the other is not, the child can feel confused by the conflict in role models unless the situation is explained to him clearly and the different possibilities are presented to him. A child's natural questions about religious and philosophical issues must be dealt with carefully. Some parents abdicate this responsibility entirely, misrepresenting these issues as unimportant and leaving the child's religious upbringing to chance or to an outsider. Jeff's father, who was not at all religious, abandoned his son to the boy's grandfather, a rabbi, for religious traning. This set up a conflict in Jeff's psyche because a solid identification with his primary role model, his father, was not possible for it lacked the religious dimension. This made it difficult for Jeff to resolve religious conflicts which concerned him later in life.

Lack of Respect

Parents whose personalities are not healthy enough to allow them to respect themselves may view their children as toys, appendages, or burdens. In *Prisoners of Childhood*, Alice Miller addresses the topic this way: "The child has a primary need to be regarded and respected as the person he really is at any given time, and as the center—the central actor—in his own activity . . . we are speaking here of a need that is narcissistic, but nevertheless legitimate, and whose fulfillment is essential for the development of a healthy self-esteem'' (p. 7). Maria Montessori writes, ''The idea that the child is a personality separate from the adult never seemed to occur to anybody. Almost all moral and philosophical thought has been oriented toward the adult, and social questions about childhood itself have never been asked. The child as a separate entity, with different needs to satisfy in order to attain the highest ends of life, has never been taken into consideration. He is seen as a weak being supported by adults, never as a human being without rights oppressed by adults'' (*The Child in the Family*, p. 15).

Norma's mother had been a narcissistically abused child, and she abused Norma as well. She was a cold, angular (stiff) person, rarely showing affection to Norma and spending most of her time, as Norma recalls, either in a depression or a frustrated rage. Her mother had little respect for herself, and she took out her emotions on Norma. When Norma did something well, she became her mother's narcissistic showpiece; the mother used her daughter's successes to boost her own self-esteem. Although Norma instinctively knew that her mother's praise and rage both had little to do with her, Norma was never respected as a person with her own needs. Her mother's needs always came first, until she finally committed suicide in front of Norma, by jumping out of a hotel window.

Bernard, too, never felt his mother respected him. He wrote of his mother's sadistic treatment:

> She loved to see me angry. I guess that was a thrill for her, to see a small person experience anger. I don't think she ever regarded my anger as valid, either because it was not her own or because I was only the child. In fact I was never regarded with as much respect as the Lilliputians were regarded by Gulliver, although I think that in her mind it was the same phenomenon—big person: toy sized person—only she could not resist her temptation to have a controllable toy at her disposal.

Sadistic parents who laugh at their children's fear or anger make their children feel stupid, unworthy or inadequate. Molly suffered from a phobia of loud noises. She would startle easily at the popping of balloons, drilling on construction sites, fireworks on the Fourth of July. Her parents, instead of helping her to relax and overcome her fear, reinforced it by making fun of it.

Numerous men and women tell of the frustration they felt when young at having their opinions and ideas treated as worthless just because the holders of these opinions were children. The parent who consistently takes the attitude "I know better than you because I'm older and I'm your parent" may give his children the lasting feeling that their views are absolutely worthless. The damage done to self-esteem in the early years of the child's development is hard to undo.

One of the most important rights within a family is the right to be listened to. Children who are scorned or ignored when they speak about what is important to them, or who grow up afraid to tell their parents anything upsetting or disturbing, have been deprived of this right. This may encourage them to lie, and will almost certainly encourage them to disparage their own ideas and feelings, just as their parents have done.

Occasionally, parents will feel that respect is something automatically due them as parents, not realizing that it is instead an integral and mutual part of the family system. A child will most likely show respect for a parent who respects him. Conversely, the parent who displays no respect for his children can expect little respect in return. Jane spoke of "continual arguments at mealtimes where Father would accuse Mother of not bringing us up properly and teaching us respect for him, and Mother would reply that it was not just *her* job, and that she should not be held responsible for everything. Father retorted that if she didn't respect him, the children wouldn't either." The problem originated in the low esteem he held for his children, thus hindering their respect for him.

The Underprotective Parent

The underprotective parent demonstrates a lack of respect and concern. This situation often emerges in a household in which one parent is tyrannical or oppressive. The child will instinctively turn to the other parent, either directly soliciting his help or indirectly asking for it by demonstrating his obvious need for it. The inadequate parent who fails to respond to this plea for help is a passive participant in the injury being perpetrated on the child by the other parent. Frank, whose father was an abusive alcoholic, got little support from his own mother even though she herself was being abused. By failing to protect herself and her children, she became her husband's accomplice. In some cases, when one parent has a tendency to smother a child, or bind him incestuously, the other parent will become a passive participant simply by trying to ignore the situation. In *Child Abuse*, the Kempes highlight this point in a discussion of incest: "Girls involved in incest often will eventually forgive their fathers, but rarely will they forgive the mothers who failed to protect them" (p. 52).

Norman felt trapped in the boarding school to which his mother had sent him. He appealed to his father for help in his plight. His father promised that if Norman would gather the appropriate information about an alternative school, he would then persuade Norman's domineering mother to allow her son to transfer. Norman did the research, but his father failed to live up to his end of the bargain, betraying his child. He was not willing to exert himself enough to help Norman escape from his mother's domination.

When children are having psychological problems, parents have a special responsibility to assist and protect them. When Olivia was nineteen, she suffered from a psychotic episode in which she had delusions and paranoid thoughts. Her parents came to the town where she was living in order to fetch her home. On the plane back, Olivia went into the bathroom, removed all her clothes, and walked out into the plane completely naked. Her father simply smiled, as it reminded him of his daughter's behavior as a child when she would call out, as she walked naked from her bath, "Nobody look, I'm coming through," thereby calling attention to herself. Something in Olivia's relationship with her parents was incestuous. This was reflected in her inappropriate behavior, and in her father's inappropriate, indulgent acceptance of her public nudity.

The underprotective parent may also fail to help the child deal with threats originating from outside sources. The consequences of this failure can be extremely serious. One boy stopped being productive in any area of his life at age thirteen, and he simply withdrew. He had a twenty-four-year-old brother living at home who was very successful. The older brother would sadistically taunt and beat up the younger brother. The parents did not intervene. They acted naively by innocently advising the boys to work out their problems between themselves. By allowing their younger child to be mistreated, they were participating in the child abuse.

Children want to be able to think that their parents will protect them. Henry's father abandoned his family when Henry was a baby and would only send them Christmas gifts. When Henry was eighteen and he visited his father, his father rejected him, telling him that he never wanted to see Henry again. However, when Henry was teased about his odd last name, he replied, "My father would break your nose for making fun of his name," which expressed his desire for a father who would protect and defend him.

Consequences of Inadequate Parenting

Edna wrote out a list of what she felt she had learned from living with an immature, tyrannical father and an inadequate mother:

> I learned—
> —To keep my anger under wraps; to be angry was to be just like my father.
>
> —To consider any and all advice from my parents as nonsense to be ignored, or defied when I was out of their sight.
>
> —To depend on friends, teachers, anyone else for warmth, approval, security; my friends seldom let me down.

—To retreat into my books, any book, all books. They couldn't find me there.

—To find any legitimate excuse to be away from home.

—To be extremely secretive at home, to say as little as I could about my life outside the home. To share none of my thoughts at all. They were used against me every time I dared.

—To never, ever let them know they'd hurt me.

A child's development can be a measure of the degree of adequacy of the parents' personalities. Parents can learn to recognize when their own weaknesses and inadequacies get in the way of their children's development. They can then assume responsibility for rectifying that situation by obtaining help from any number of outer sources, such as a psychotherapist or counselor.

The Devouring Parent

The Smothering Parent

Devouring parents bind up their children's energy, leaving them no strength to grow and develop their unique personalities. They smother their children with rules and demands, overprotective love and guilt. These parents will go to great lengths to be sure that their children do not undergo the necessary separation-individuation process and have independent lives. The smothering parent will overinvest in a child, making huge sacrifices and commitments but expecting the child's life and soul in return. *I want you all for myself* is the underlying theme; the devouring parent desperately craves his child's love and attention.

Parents who refuse to let their children separate from them are actually restricting and limiting their children's potential to make something of themselves in the world.

If a parent treats his child as a friend who will comfort the parent when he is upset, or as a *confidante*, the child is being abused. A daughter's primary role ought not to be to make her father feel good and to listen to the sexual problems he is having with her mother (or any other woman).

Linda's father begged her for letters, saying that they gave his depressed spirit a lift. He could not go on without them, he said. Then he went on to insist that she be religiously devout for his sake. Later she was asked to lend a large amount of money to her brother, so she borrowed it from a bank and gave it to her brother in order to please her father. In effect, she had become her father's *confidante*, surrogate wife, and family benefactor. In time she came to realize that it was vital for her to learn to separate from her father's demands and pressures.

Another girl who was her father's favorite was told repeatedly to make sure she did not do the things her mother had done. In this way, the father was trying to get his daughter to compensate for the inadequate relationship he had with his wife. He was also making it nearly impossible for her to identify with her own mother. Emily, too, was placed in the role of protector and servant to her father. Her mother had grown tired of her husband and said to Emily, "He's your father—you take care of him." Emily was expected to cook, clean house, and keep her father happy.

There are a number of examples of this kind of smothering in U.S. history. Thomas Jefferson had a similar kind of smothering style. His love and concern for his daughters grew excessive; to be happy he seemed to need their constant care and affection. In a letter to Martha (March 28, 1787), he says, "Nobody in the world can make me so happy, or so miserable as you." Another such example was written ten years later in a letter to his daughter Maria (March 11, 1797), "My love to your sister and yourself knows no bounds, and as I scarcely see any other object in life, so I would quit it with desire whenever my continuance in it shall become useless to you."

A clue to Jefferson's smothering style with his children may be found in his own background and in his decision to live at Monticello. Monticello was only four miles away from his mother, and his failure to be geographically mobile led to his financial stagnation in the Virginia countryside, since he could not earn enough money from his law practice there. Jefferson missed having the constant affection and attention for which he obviously hungered. He loved his daughters with the kind of intensity and need usually reserved for a wife. He expected to come first in everyone's affection, and the message that he unconsciously transmitted to his daughters was "Above all, always be available for me." In turn, their first concern was for their father, not for themselves or their own families. Their personal lives were disastrous. Thomas Jefferson went on to become the President of the United States—with his daughter Martha as his First Lady. His needs cancelled those of his children.

A young man named Brad wrote about his sadistic mother,

> I remember my early life being filled with frustration. There was the duality of my feeling for my mother—on one hand I loved her, and on the other, I wanted to hit her and stop her from restricting me. She would hold me and kiss me in the most sadistic manner in the sense that when I tried to get away she wouldn't let me go and would hold me until I screamed or laughed in anger.

Brad's father left when Brad was three, and his mother's actions clearly indicate an incestuous, possessive attitude toward her son. Brad felt that she did not want to lose her son, this second man in her life.

When children sense a parent's loneliness or depression, they will often try to fill in the gap. They feel that they have to humor their parents, to protect them, and they often feel hesitant about separating from the parent who has tried to bind them. They are overly concerned about their parents being devastated by the rejection when they leave home and their parents are alone.

When parents have an incestuous style, they do not want to face the idea that their children will grow up and direct their sexuality toward people outside the family. Many fathers find having a daughter a very satisfying and rewarding experience until that child enters adolescence. Adolescence brings unique pressures to the father's role; he must deal with his daughter's sexuality, and he must curb any incestuous thoughts he may have. It may be easier for this kind of father if he can convince his daughter to live like a nun, because then he never really has to separate from her sexuality, since it will be repressed. Fathers whose daughters don't want to act like nuns sometimes feel the desire to lock up their children "for their own safety." They see their children's exploratory sexual behavior as promiscuity or whoring. There is a tremendous investment of pathologically binding jealousy in these situations; the smothering parent is severely disturbing the family system by saying he can't trust it.

Smothering parents panic at the thought of having their children move away. Jung speaks of mothers "who find their sole meaning in their children and imagine they will sink into a bottomless void when they have to give them up" (*CW*, Vol. 7, p. 79). Carol's parents never encouraged her to move out of the family home, and would inadvertently discourage her from taking the necessary steps to separate from them. They would say, "Sure you can move out—when you marry," or "Only 'those kinds of girls' move out on their own." Carol would from time to time venture out, but each time she felt compelled to move back.

Even if they do leave, these children are expected to visit their parents constantly. During their college years, they are required to spend all of their vacations back home. The parents also act "territorial" and get very hurt if their children do not stop by each time they are in the area.

The smothering parent assumes that a child's mistakes will trap him for life, and so he will try to manage a child's life in such a way that the child will accept his parents' attitudes about the world directly instead of developing his own.

One young boy stated to me proudly that his mother would do *anything* for him. But a positive parent will never do for his child what that child can do for himself. Over-assisting a child is not really assisting him at all.

A parent who smothers his child may feel he is merely protecting that child from harm and disappointment. When this desire to protect goes too far, however, it can severely limit the child's choices in the world. Mary's parents were anxious to protect her. Any time a venture of hers did not work out, they would say "See what happened?" or "See where that got you?" They did not want her to try anything new. They encouraged in Mary the attitude "It can always be worse" rather than "It could be even better."

The parent who blocks the development of his child may be

blocking his own development as well. The flexible parent will grow with his child and celebrate that child's healthy development and the discoveries she makes as she grows.

The Manager

Some parents feel it is important to lead their children rather than follow them. They practice "precision" parenting in their children's lives, spouting such aphorisms as "All rules must be followed to the letter," and "Father/Mother knows best." The parent who acts as a manager for his child will not be likely to recognize that, in most cases, it is the child who knows best.

A child growing up with a manager for a parent hears a steady barrage of commands, orders and suggestions about anything and everything; what foods to eat, what books to read, what college to attend, what person to marry—and so on. These parents are always several steps ahead of their children. If the child is in medical school, the parents are already planning the decoration of his office, unmindful of the fact that he may plan to go into research or teaching or some other field, since they have decided he will open up a practice.

Louise was a typical manager-parent who lived in an upper-middle-class suburb. She was overly sensitive and outer-directed, and couldn't stand to have anything in her home or her life out of order. She had to be in control at all times. She ran her house like a boarding school or a summer camp, where every moment is planned in advance. She set so many limits that the children were not able to move. Her son was forced to play the instrument she selected, and he had to practice every afternoon. If he didn't practice, he was not allowed to play with his friends. The children had to read a book a week—she suggested the books—and to report on their reading each week for her. Time for homework was specified each day. The children were not permitted to break this orderly routine.

Louise *gloried* in reading books about the devoted mothers of famous children. She fancied herself quite devoted and prided herself on having the family so well-organized. But the results were quite different from what she expected. Her son became self-destructive, constantly getting hurt and having to go to the hospital emergency room. He was sadistic to teachers and other children in his class and was often in trouble at school.

Another manager-mother decreed that at five o'clock every evening, her daughters had to take out their needlework. If her children were late for supper, they had to fix their own. If they were upstairs when she called them to the dinner table and they didn't come down immediately, she wouldn't feed them. One of her daughters rebelled by developing anorexia. Her illness was a desperate attempt to get out from under her mother's management.

Although these cases are more harsh than most, they reflect a tendency many parents display in dealing with their children. The parents are so anxious that the child be accomplished and successful that they end up turning play into work. Tom was only a mediocre violinist, but his mother wanted him to be great. In order to get Tom's violin teacher to like her, she donated money to the teacher's favorite charity. She recorded all the concerts at which her child played as if to document his life for posterity. She was always pressuring Tom, and claimed that he would later thank her for all of this persistent attention. But because he was forced into it, a child like Tom will in fact be more likely to give up his musical studies.

Some cultures seem to encourage inflexible, rigid managerial styles of parenting, the idea being that things run more smoothly under autocratic rule. One of my patients described an example of this formal style in her childhood in Germany. In her household, rules regarding table manners were strictly enforced. Children were not to talk at the table unless they were addressed first. Children were not to begin eating until the adults had begun. A child was under no circumstances to interrupt an adult. No child was allowed to stand up until the meal was over. The message my patient perceived behind all these rules was that children had nothing to offer adults, and that, if allowed to act as they pleased, children would create a *madhouse*. Children were not treated with respect, as equal members of the family system.

Manager-parents will sometimes try to dictate their children's professions, even going so far as to give them a helping hand to push them in the right direction. Brian's father was a famous physician on the faculty of a medical school. Brian applied to medical schools but didn't get in, but he did get into dental school. He felt pleased about that, and planned to go into dentistry. One day his father called him aside and informed him that he had pulled some strings, and Brian had now been accepted into medical school. For the first time in his life, Brian had felt that he had achieved something on his own, and now his father was taking that feeling away from him. His father failed to appreciate that Brian valued his admission to dental school as a personal achievement. With the help of analysis, he was able to inform his father that he would not go to medical school. He ended up being a dentist, and found his work rewarding.

Other children are not able to disengage themselves so neatly. They are coerced into entering the family business and working for their parents, instead of striking out on their own. Parents who are successful and rich often have a lot of power in influencing their children's decisions. When there is money in the family, there may be a tendency for the parent to "buy" the child. Trade-offs, sometimes far from subtle, are arranged: "I will give you all the money you need, and a fancy car, if you will go to the college I choose."

Margaret married into a wealthy family, and she and her husband bought a house in a nice suburb. Her new father-in-law then demanded—not suggested—that they remodel the kitchen. It mattered to him, and he controlled the money in the family. Margaret's husband had not yet separated sufficiently from his parents, so he acquiesced to their smothering demands, and it cost him his marriage. Some devouring parents develop a style in which the money is doled out only in small amounts. There is an implied or explicit threat—if you don't comply, you'll lose the inheritance or the trust fund. Managers have no faith in their children making the right decisions themselves. They are unable to follow their children or to let them take their own risks.

Respect for Privacy

Smothering parents have little respect for the privacy or sanctity of their children's possessions, secrets, letters, or bodies. They often feel they have a special parental license to ask any questions they please and to demand emotional and physical openness from their children. Not only is this a violation of the child's right to privacy; it is also a sign of the parents' desire to possess the child.

The nosy parent feels no hesitancy about invading his child's privacy by reading the child's mail and diaries, by listening in on telephone conversations, even—as was the case with one woman I knew—by hypnotizing their children. The most common example of this kind of invasion is the "open door" policy. Paula, as a twelve-year-old, couldn't understand the transformation of her parents' attitude toward her. Up until that time, they had had a permissive attitude toward her visiting friends and her goings and comings. As soon as she approached adolescence, though, all of this changed:

> It felt like all of a sudden, they were all over me. All doors had to be open at all times; my mail and telephone calls were being monitored very closely. I felt as if I were under twenty-four hour surveillance. They wanted to know where I was at all times.

She correlated her parents' constant surveillance with her developing compulsion to lie. Paula's parents managed to justify their actions to themselves by saying that they were only making sure she wasn't getting into trouble. For a number of years as an adult, Paula went through a promiscuous period. She was basically frigid in her adventures, but she seemed driven to repeat them. She underwent therapy in part because, after two years of marriage, she had lost all interest in sex. As it turned out, her sexual aversion was a means of asserting that she had control over her own body, a right that her parents had always denied her.

The results for Paula were devastating: her ability to achieve sexual pleasure was almost nonexistent, and her difficulty with regard to sexual fantasies was connected to the loss of much of her sexual drive. If sexual pleasure is partly dependent on the ability to fantasize, then inhibiting of sexual fantasies (by depriving a child of his necessary privacy) means the parent is inhibiting the possibility of sexual pleasure. Paula felt guilty if she did fantasize, and she suppressed her actual fantasies in an attempt to direct her fantasy life. By thwarting her privacy, Paula's parents helped thwart her *psychosexual* development. Privacy is not a luxury; privacy is a necessity. And when Paula was an adult, even though her parents were no longer actively thwarting her, she suffered from an internalized image of her parents' restrictive attitudes. It was only after she worked through these complexes that she was able to visualize herself as a mother, and make the decision to start her own family.

One patient who grew up in a household with restrictions on locked doors took refuge in closets in order to have privacy. The result of her parents' "progressive" rule about openness was that one of the children became an exhibitionist, and the other had a body which looked collapsed inward. In such houses, the scene has not been properly set for the healthy development of the children. Children's doors should have locks on them, and children should be assured that they are entitled to their privacy. Parents may unwittingly neglect such "details" of their children's physical environments, not realizing how important the setting becomes in the child's maturation.

When Wendy was seventeen, her mother advised her to take birth control pills. Then when she visited her father, her step-mother found the pills in her luggage. The stepmother took every opportunity to talk about the pills' horrible side effects. Although she disguised it as helpful concern, her attitude was simply nosy and inappropriate. It was an invasion of privacy for her to go through the luggage, and it was a further betrayal to make private information public.

Some parents invade their children's privacy to the extent that they claim the right to control their children's fantasy lives. Such parents are making a fundamental error in their assessments, as they should realize that fantasy is not reality—children are not necessarily going to act out their fantasies. The parents' desire to intervene and control the child's fantasy life gets in the way of children working out personal issues through the medium of fantasy. Cheryl and Peter would listen to their eleven-year-old son's telephone conversations, and once heard him talking to a twelve-year-old friend. The boys were sharing a sexual fantasy. Cheryl and Peter were outraged and decided to intervene. This kind of "protection" and interference destroys the trust in the parent/child relationship. Children have a right to their private lives, especially to their fantasies, and should not have to justify them to their parents.

Overprotectiveness

When my son was eleven years old, he came home one day with a swollen toe which eventually proved to be broken. A rock had fallen on his foot while he was out playing. I must have conveyed some sign of concern which he interpreted as "Why aren't you more careful?" or "Is this a sign that you are accident-prone?" My son informed me that if a child has not broken one bone by the time he reaches the age of fourteen, he must have broken a world record.

If a child cannot risk breaking a bone once in a while, he will not participate in most games, will stay off bicycles and roller skates, and will most definitely shy away from all contact sports. However, the real danger of the child identifying with his parents' overprotective attitude is evidenced later in life, when that child may be relegated to a life of mediocrity well below his actual potential. This seemingly innocuous overprotectiveness can doom a child to being an underachiever.

The overprotective parent transmits to the child the notion that to experience life's possibilities is to subject oneself to unnecessary risk. Don't ride a bike: you will get into an accident. Don't drive a car until you are in your twenties: it is statistically too dangerous. Don't go in the deep water: you may drown. Well-meaning parents can be full of such overprotective advice: "Don't ever use a public toilet." "Don't ever talk to a stranger." "Always expect the worst; then you'll never be disappointed." All of these are negative views of life in general, but this last warning is particularly dangerous because it can become a self-fulfilling prophecy—a curse—as the child grows up expecting people to abuse him, to disappoint him, to abandon him. In trying to protect the child from hurt, the parents are actually setting him up for a far more painful situation.

Scott remembered feeling left out of normal social exchanges. His mother was always afraid of the consequences of his contact with other children. Scott recalled,

> I was always a peripheral person for this reason. I never had first-hand experience with other children. I would hear about things they had done either from them or from my mother, but never participated. She would never let me. If I did find a playmate, she would find some way to discourage me. I shut myself off, and from then on my confidence was shaky and I had no plan of attack in life.

Some parents are overprotective because they sincerely do not want their children to have to face problems with which they themselves were confronted when they were young. Jonathan could never understand, for example, why his father shielded his sister from him. He acted as though Jonathan were a criminal or a bully who would hurt her if given the chance. It was only later that Jonathan learned that his father had been abused, as a child, by an older brother. He acted as though the children in any family were dangerous to one another. Jonathan's father could not see the potential for a healthy love between his own children and didn't permit the development of affectionate interactions in his children's relationships.

Worrying is also a waste of energy, because it doesn't accomplish anything. If a parent is not in a position to help a child in a specific situation, he should trust that the child will be fine, and then deal with any problems that come up if they do arise. When parents interrupt their children's lives with worry, they seem to be functioning as if they are waiting for the end of the world or some inevitable catastrophe to strike. They have what Fritz Perls has called "catastrophic expectations." They are transmitting a lack of confidence in their children's ability to get along in the world.

There are many paradoxical messages that overprotective parents present to their children. They may consciously want their children to develop healthily, "get married and give us grandchildren"—but then they want their adult children to visit often, telephone even more frequently, and generally keep the parent-child bond tight. They are giving with one hand and taking away with the other, asking their children to be independent adults and yet not giving them the power to be independent.

One woman told me, "My mother did everything for me. She even bathed me until I was twelve." As an unfortunate consequence, this young woman never learned how to take care of her body or her possessions. She was a successful executive, but she neglected her health, lost track of her belongings, allowed her home to get messier and messier, and failed to pay her bills. Since her mother had done everything for her, she never learned how to assume responsibility on her own. Parents who keep their children from being autonomous do them a great disservice, since these children will flounder in the outside world. The lack of survival knowledge can also be embarrassing. This same woman was once called at work by her maid, who thought that someone had broken into the house because there were clothes and possessions strewn all over the floor, drawers were open and spilling their contents, and so forth. But no break-in had occurred; this woman's home always looked like that.

William had a very strong dependence on both his mother and his father. His attachment to his mother effectively kept him from having successful relationships with women, and he maintained his status of dependency. He was often impotent, and had a recurring dream of trying to shoot people with a gun that would not go off. It was only when he began to try to strike out on his own and make decisions for himself that he began to work through this syndrome.

Another young man I knew sensed that his mother was too close; she devalued his potential in the world and would have preferred that he remain attached to her. She wanted to keep track of him all the time, and she dictated his every move. Since, as he felt, his mother had a grip on his sexuality, he was not successful in his relationships with women and eventually became a transvestite. Although his case is extreme, it demonstrates an important element of the syndrome of overprotectiveness. The overprotected child may feel that his parents have all his energy and he may feel the need to make some drastic move away from his parents to escape their domination so that his own personality can develop properly.

The Martyr

The role of the martyr is sometimes taken on by the smothering parent, making sure the child is aware of all that he has given up for the child. Kate thought that being a mother meant giving up one's career and all of one's hopes of autonomy, since that is what she perceived her mother as having done. She associated her mother's chronic alcoholism with her depression which developed when she abandoned her career in order to be a full-time mother. Now Kate is firmly determined not to have children of her own. In her mind, having children is associated with sickness, sacrifice, and psychological disorder.

Alison's parents used to state that "everything was all right until you children were born," and "we used to be so happy until . . . " There are few things so depressing for a child as a mother who feels she has sacrificed her life for her child, regardless of whether she transmits this verbally or nonverbally.

Laurie's mother would induce guilt by representing herself to her neighbors and friends as persecuted and neglected. Laurie once received a letter of complaint from a friend of her mother, saying "How can you stand by and not help your mother pay for the heat and the repairs on her home?" The implication was that she was a cruel, ungrateful child, when actually, her mother could afford her own repairs better than Laurie could, and was simply trying to get her daughter to feel guilty for not paying enough attention to her.

The harried housewife is a classic example of the martyr who refuses to delegate responsibility within the family. She may continually complain that no one helps her out—but she does nothing to change the situation. Judy's mother was this kind of martyr. While she was married, she felt that she had sacrificed everything for her husband and children. She would wear the same coat for seven years, and would remind everyone that she was depriving herself for them. Once she complained that no one ever helped her prepare holiday dinners, so the next holiday eve, Judy came over to help. Her mother said to her, "No, I don't need any help; I'd rather do it myself." When Judy's father had a love affair, her mother felt betrayed; she professed surprise and anger as her "perfect" marriage came apart. She would not acknowledge that she had any part in the disintegration of her relationship with her husband, preferring to suffer in a nonworking marriage than to get a divorce. She was bound to suffer, no matter what it cost her. She paid for part of Judy's wedding—and then never let Judy forget it. She also loaned Judy and her husband $2,000 for a down payment on their home, without any mention of a time limit for repayment. When Judy and her husband subsequently went on vacation, her mother complained "So, you have money for a trip—where's my money?" In classic martyr fashion, she was begrudging Judy her happiness.

Parents sacrifice a lot of time, energy and money to their children, but most of them are not martyrs. Caring parents are able to handle the paradox of offering what they have without sacrificing who they are. It is when the sacrifice is seen as meaningless, or when it becomes masochistically fulfilling for the parent, that it becomes a burden for parent and child alike.

The Tyrannical Parent

King of the Hill

Parents who are struggling with low self-esteem will often try to compensate for this deficiency by tyrannizing other family members. The tyrannical parent displays a cruel, inflexible, often outrageous style in dealing with his children. His moods fluctuate wildly, and every member of his household is expected to bow down to him and try to grant his wishes. He may see himself, or his children may see him, as King of the Hill, or in the case of mothers, Queen Bee. The tyrannical parent often has narcissistic disturbances; his needs are not adequately being met, and so he compensates for this by terrorizing his children. The children grow up in an atmosphere of mistrust and fear.

A house is meant for the whole family to live in, not just the parents. Fred never wanted to have parties in his parents' house because he had observed what had happened at his brother's parties. His parents would get so nervous over what was going on that they would constantly interrupt. The guests would feel uncomfortable and go home early. When decorating, many parents unconsciously create an unlivable home. An example of this is the decor-in-white, where a person must dust himself off before he sits on the furniture. Often parents who choose delicate furnishings are self-centered, creating rooms just for themselves with no regard for their children.

Some tyrannical parents actually betray and defraud their children. When Andrew was twenty-one, he needed $2,000 to

71

buy a car. His father told him to borrow $5,000 from the bank, saying that he could use the $3,000 from the loan and would be responsible for repaying it. Andrew found out later that he had a bad credit rating because his father had failed to make the loan payments. Another time, Andrew gave his father $800 so that his father could purchase some stocks for him. When Andrew saw that his stock had gone up twenty points, he decided to sell and asked his father to get the money for him. His father then admitted that he had never bought the stock in the first place; he had simply put the money into his own business.

The Tyranny of Moods

Domineering parents often set up a "tyranny of moods" in their households. Many parents preface their demands with statements such as: "As long as you live under my foof . . . ," or "You don't have the right to be unhappy in my house." When their child seems upset, they will say, "Smile!" instead of asking what the problem is. Kathy's father always told her "Be happy. As long as you're happy, I'm happy." According to Kathy, there was always a dispute about the criteria for happiness. What made her happy did not seem to match what made him happy. She also felt that while she was in his home she couldn't express or share any other condition but happiness, and this restriction carried over into her other relationships. Her father taught her to bottle up her own feelings in order to keep harmony in his house. He did not want to be empathetic with her inner self and her needs.

The tyrannical parent will at times enslave his children, feeling that he himself is the only one working hard. He may not realize that the child has work of his own to do. Even if the child is a full-time student, plays a musical instrument, is involved with sports and does small chores around the house, his parents may complain that he is not doing any work. Some children are expected to clean the entire house, or cook all the meals. Their own need for time to themselves is not taken into account. One young daughter spent her evenings waiting on her father. She was expected to meet him at the bus stop and walk him home, help cook the meal and wash the dishes, entertain him after dinner. He would get hurt if she had anything else she wanted to do in the evenings. Such children are given responsibility, but are denied the power and the motivation to progress in their own lives.

Gina's mother, whose moods fluctuated constantly, would make swift and erratic changes in the way she ran the household. For example, one day she suddenly decided that she no longer wanted to prepare meals for her daughter. This left Gina literally and figuratively looking for nourishment. Similarly, Maria was brought up within a tyrannical family structure where the father's moods determined the family's well-being. She grew up in a chronic state of fear that she would be "stepping on father's toes" if she expressed any criticism of the family, her father in particular. She said that she felt like an animal caught in a trap. Lydia's mother would sweetly take Lydia shopping and select clothes for her, but if Lydia didn't like her selections, the mother would burst out screaming in the middle of the store, "You ungrateful child!"

Moods are sometimes used as weapons by parents. A child who lives in fear of his parent's chronic bad tempers, blow-ups or tantrums is being forced to undergo "emotional whipping." These children usually feel that they have been unfairly punished for infractions they have not committed.

Often children feel they cannot even fight back. Diane told me of one holiday when she worked very hard to prepare a beautiful feast. It was a pleasant evening, she said, and her tyrannical father was for once being charming. But as soon as the guests had left "he exploded, calling me a lazy bitch and everything else he could think of. I'd failed to scrub the bathroom, how could I think of bringing in guests? There was no way to win."

Tyranny is often backed up by the threat of physical violence. When these threats are carried out, the child may feel that his life and safety are endangered. When Lee was eight, he bumped into his father when running past him. His father, Lee said, "responded like a madman" and gave him a beating. Other parents will make the threats, raising their hands as if ready to strike, but not actually hitting their children. In this way, they can defend themselves against the allegation of abuse by noting how few times they have "touched" the child. However, these "controlled" parents are often suppressing their rage and then periodically manifesting their feelings of anger by chronic outbursts of verbal and emotional abuse. The child and his parents live in a state of cold war, with the threat of greater destruction always beneath the surface and ready to burst through. Children in this situation are often obedient, but terrified, feeling that they can never trust their parents because it is never clear how the parents will react.

The more subtle psychological tyranny is the tyranny of moods, in which a parent will say such things as "Don't talk to me now, can't you see how I'm feeling?" "Shut up," or "Don't talk to Daddy tonight; he's had a hard day at the office." The child's freedom of expression—especially of angry feelings or criticism—is severely restricted. In *The Golden Cage*, Hilde Bruch tells of one girl in such a situation: "When a question was raised about expressing anger, she answered with bitterness, 'I'm never allowed to! My mother wouldn't stand for it. I'm not allowed to talk back or anything like that' " (p. 32).

Lisa grew up in terror, afraid that her father would beat her for any real or imagined misdemeanor. She said,

> His moods were violent and totally unpredictable. The family's fate for the week might rest on the outcome of a basketball game. Anything could set him off; he'd have screaming battles with telephone operators and actually broke the phone throwing it across the room. There were some deliberate beatings, some of them in public, but the rages were even more frightening. At the end of a meal he'd loosen his belt. I was never sure if he was making himself comfortable or getting ready to use it on me. I think now I've forgotten the actual beatings and only remember the fear.

Her mother participated passively in this tyranny by failing to defend Lisa from her husband's irrational attacks.

Cruel and Outrageous Treatment

Parents who carry their tyranny to extremes are often guilty of physical child abuse—beatings, burnings, severe neglect—that leave the child scarred, physically and emotionally, for life. These parents may be suffering from delusional psychoses ("God told me to beat my child"); they may be aggressively sociopathic people who can communicate their desires and frustrations only by hitting their children; they may be fanatically religious or simply so severely troubled themselves that they cannot control their violent behavior.

Darlene was a prostitute, and she had clearly been set up for that kind of life by her mother's outrageous, enslaving demands. When Darlene was small, she had to serve as her mother's confidante as her mother told her perverted stories of her own sexual life. Her stepfather abused her sexually. Darlene ran away from home and became a prostitute at fifteen. When she got back in touch with her mother, her mother begged her for money, which Darlene then sent. From then on, even when she wanted to stop prostituting herself, she felt she couldn't because her mother kept asking her for money. Although she knew how Darlene was earning the money, her mother continued to exploit her child's natural desire to help her out.

Even when the behavior is not so extreme, the tyrannical parent will often treat his children sadistically, taunting them and berating them for not being able to take the malicious comments. Though the cruelty may be presented as teasing, or as a passing, casual comment, children usually understand the unconscious messages of rejection underlying the parent's words. Andrea's father would say to his children, "We should have had pigs instead of you children." And one parent I know said to her daughter, "Martha, what would you like for Christmas—oh, but come to think of it, I can't afford to get you a present this year. Maybe next year." Martha's mother would never call Martha on holidays, but would always call Martha's sister. When Martha would finally call her mother, her mother would casually report that she had just talked to Martha's sister. In a similarly unfeeling fashion, Stuart's mother once gave him a piece of advice and then added, "You're old enough and ugly enough to know that." When Stuart asked her why she had said that, she said, "I don't know. My mother always said it to me."

Many parents fail to recognize the importance of helping a child feel comfortable with the way he or she looks. In making fun of a child's looks, or in refusing to correct deformities—failing to provide braces for a child with badly crooked teeth, for example —the parent is completely negating the importance of the cosmetic side of life, and giving the child a handicap in his social development.

When Karen had a "sweet sixteen" party she went to the beauty parlor as a special treat and returned feeling lovely, only to have her father launch into an attack on her new hairstyle. She felt that he couldn't stand to see her looking pretty, that he was only comfortable with her so long as she was homely. He felt threatened by her attractiveness to other men, and was unable to validate her as a growing woman. She thus had a hard time accepting herself as a sexual being. She gained a good deal of weight and for years felt certain that she was unattractive.

Inflexibility and Hypocrisy

Tyrannical parents may be inflexible or hypocritical, expecting their children to do everything perfectly. The parents, however, feel they have the right to make mistakes themselves.

One father who had a two-and-a-half-year-old daughter had a tendency to fly off the handle. During one summer storm, all of the peas in his garden were blown down. When the storm ended, he and his daughter went into the garden, and he started screaming and cursing at the fate of his peas. After a few minutes of this, he heard his daughter imitating him, cursing in the same style. He was shocked and he yelled at her, not realizing that the child had acted thus because she felt threatened. She thought she had a madman for a father, and she was simply mimicking him. In a sense, at less than three years old she was already acting as a therapist for her father, mirroring back to him his immature behavior.

Hypocritical parents may encourage double standards of behavior. Those who tacitly accept their chidlren's sexuality outside the home but go into a rage if the child brings a boyfriend or girlfriend home to spend the night, often are attempting to put up a good façade in front of friends and neighbors. Such hypocrisy is often motivated by the parents' inability to confront their child's developing sexuality.

David realized that his father was completely inflexible and harsh in his dealings with his children as a result of his insecurity and fear of his children's rejection. He thought they would discard him if he was not firm. David's father, like many tyrannical parents, equated flexibility with weakness. In reality, the ability to be flexible is a strength.

Consequences of Tyrannical Behavior

The child who grows up with a tyrant for a parent will almost inevitably bear deep scars from the psychological—and physical—battles. Some children will repeat the family curse and tyrannize their own children. Others will always be looking for unattainable love and affection from cruel, manipulative people similar to the tyrannical parent.

Usually the child will feel weakened through his encounters with the tyrant. Kent always felt drained in the presence of his father, who was an excellent material provider but a poor emotional provider. Kent found that he hated calling his father on the telephone. He made the observation that his father never called him, and when Kent called, his father would act as though he weren't even listening. He realized that his basic insecurity in relationships came from the fear that people didn't want to be with him. His father brought on this reaction by his hostility toward Kent.

Lisa found that she got involved with men who treated her as her father had. They were critical and icy, rejecting her or terrorizing her, and inhibiting her emotional and physical pleasures. She had a compulsive need to seek out their affection, and the more they rejected her, the more she advanced her relationships toward them.

Often a child will rebel against tyranny by doing what is most forbidden. If a child becomes promiscuous, it could reflect the parents' fierce denial of sex. These rebellions are often self-destructive. After Bonnie left her father's house, in an attempt to assert her individuality, she decided to marry a man her parents did not approve of. She really didn't love him and came to realize that her self-destructive marriage to the wrong mate was a response to her father's example. Her father had been the moody tyrant and her mother had been his slave, catering to his moods. This set the response pattern for the rest of the family members. But Bonnie, having rebelled, was trapped, married to a man she didn't like but wouldn't divorce, and afraid to seek meaningful employment out of fear that her husband would feel threatened by it.

Though a tyrannical parent often recognizes his tyranny, he may simply not be able to control it. The first step is for the tyrant to recognize the counterproductive nature of his attitude within the family system. Often with professional help, he can learn to treat his family members as human beings worthy of respect, and can eventually modify this devastating trait which can, if unchecked, prove one of the most debilitating family curses.

*From Generation Unto Generation:
Repeating the Family Curse*

Money Matters

The Psychological Reality of Money

To the average individual in our society money is a necessity, and its acquisition comes to be extremely important. The way a child comes to relate to money can have a profound effect on other areas of his life. The ancient Greeks realized this when they correlated the absence of money with the disease process, and the presence of money with the cure.

Today many children are concerned about their stations in life, often wishing they could change economic classes and achieve the good life that they imagine only money can buy. Parents need to encourage their children to develop a realistic attitude toward monetary matters.

A strong notion handed down from generation to generation in Western civilization holds that affluence leads to decadence and the denial of the spirit. We are all familiar with the quote: *Money is the root of all evil*. In full it reads as follows:

> They that desire to be rich fall into a temptation and a snare and many foolish and hurtful lusts, such as drown men in destruction and perdition. For the love of money is the root of all kinds of evil: which some reaching after have been led astray from the faith: and have pierced themselves through with many sorrows. (1 Timothy, 6:9–10)

The Puritan work ethic allows only for hard work and self-sacrifice. It mandates that one should earn what one has by the

81

sweat of one's brow, and that there should be no shortcuts, no easy way to wealth. Being in debt is frowned upon; so are idle hands. These precepts are commonly transferred from parents to their children. But in our society, this is often not a realistic attitude.

To underestimate one's credit potential is to underestimate one's assets. The failure to understand this reflects a neurosis with regard to money, because it means living beneath one's potential. Part of the art of dealing with money is knowing how and when to go into debt, so that one can obtain the maximum potential from the money one borrows. As Benjamin Franklin said, "Money can beget money." Many people—Thomas Jefferson was a prime example—live fruitful, creative lives without a lot of cash on hand. Jefferson was often in debt, but he lived to his fullest potential. This goes against the ethic which encourages us to save rather than to borrow. The person who will only save, who will not take risks with his money or his security, who sees a concern with money as crass or dark or shady, will not succeed with money and will not pass on to his children a healthy, creative attitude toward money.

Often the root of the family neurosis stems from some irresponsible treatment of the family's assets. For instance, one eighty-year-old millionaire married a fortune-hunter after his first wife died. When he died a few years later, all of his money went to his new wife. This situation disrupted the entire family system. How some parents deal with their possessions can also demonstrate irresponsibility. I knew a man who was having trouble with his Rolls Royce, so he simply gave it to a garage. This same man owned one of the few private castles left in England, and was so discouraged by the expenses of running it that he sold it for a price substantially lower than its market value, not considering the best interests of his heirs. A parent who flies to Las Vegas and "drops a hundred thousand" in a craps game is similarly irresponsible. These parents fail to realize that their assets are an integral part of their family systems, and should not be disposed of lightly.

Neither should the assets of a family be hoarded at the expense of the family system. One parent I know refused to use any of his inherited money to send his children to college, since the ethic he had learned as a child demanded that inherited money be passed on intact to the next generation, with none of the principal (and preferably none of the interest) spent within the family system.

Children of millionaires often have to carry the burden of their parents' wealth. The parents may consciously or unconsciously view their own acquisition of money as shady, so although they may pass their money on, they also pass on ambivalent, paradoxical attitudes toward it. Some of the destructive tendencies of children from wealthy families may stem from this unconscious identification. The children have the task of coming to terms with the acquisition of money, even if they themselves never had to acquire it.

The mishandling of money can also cause trouble in the child's adjustment. One boy named John was shy and introverted. He needed a push, but it never came. He lacked the energy even to ask for money. He knew his father had it, and he knew his father wouldn't give it to him. John's father was a millionaire, and John was a do-nothing until the age of fifty when his inheritance came. By then it was too late.

This kind of problem stems from the lack of a realistic attitude about the need to acquire money in this society. Among the important ideas parents need to impart to a child about money, two stand out. One is that money is never freely given away; everything has its price. Another is that one should never depend on inherited money; you have to make your own opportunities. This often requires flexibility (for example, being geographically mobile).

The Resourceful Child

The child needs to be taught to recognize the realistic need for money in this society, and then be helped to marshall all of his resources to reach his goals. The lack of money is often correlated with the lack of flexibility in life; it can cut down on geographic mobility as well as cause a kind of psychic paralysis. But the resourceful child is aware of the power structure of his world and learns to work within it. He is also aware of his opportunities. Part of the key to being successful in this world is to understand the rules by which one has to operate. The criminal evades paying taxes; the resourceful person finds tax shelters. Resourceful people are conscious of the formal laws of their society; they are also aware of custom and culture.

Encouraging Creative Ingenuity

Looking for possibilities in chance occurrences can help one to realize one's potential in life. It is important for children to consider the fairness of exchanges within the family system. Most children are expected to help around the house as part of their contribution to the system. But for special tasks, they should be encouraged to negotiate what their services are worth.

How can one generate creative cleverness in a child? When this trait makes an appearance in the child's behavior—in his creative problem solving, in his sense of humor and his stories—it can be recognized and positively reinforced. Parents can encourage the child in this basic part of his personality.

Gift Exchanges and Use of Assets

Gift exchanges are important. When an unfair exchange takes place, the delicate balance of money and power is disrupted. Gift giving can often be a problem area between parents and children. Roberta was subjected to a gift-related maneuver in which the gift, or the absence of one, is used to convey a specific message to a child. When Roberta spent Christmas with her new husband instead of her mother, her mother pretended to be cheerful about it. But when it came time for the traditional exchange of presents, Roberta received nothing. She was, of course, supposed to be awash with pity for her lonely mother. Instead she felt manipulated by her mother's selfishness.

Some parents openly appropriate the money that actually belongs to their children. I first recognized this pattern when Jeff related how his parents had kept all of the money he had been given for his Bar Mitzvah. Later he found out that his father had kept the money Jeff's grandfather had saved for him—money sent expressly to pay for Jeff's tuition in graduate school. Some parents cash in their child's bonds (held in the name of both parents and child) without the child's permission—bonds originally intended to pay for the child's education.

Jackie had a similar shock when she realized the nature of a "gift" she had been given. Her father came to her one day to tell her that he had just bought a car for her. At first she was annoyed because she would have liked to have been part of the decision-making process. But she decided that since the car was a generous gift on her father's part, she should accept it gracefully. She was later informed, to her surprise, that the money he had used to purchase the car was actually her own money that had been left to her by her grandmother. Jackie's annoyance at this deception came out clearly in a dream:

> My sister and I got into my car (a Volkswagen bug) and I tried to get the car out of the parking lot in back of my old house . . . but there were several cars blocking it. The main car that was blocking it was my father's—a shiny red Mercedes. He walked over, and I pointed out that his car was blocking us but he kept insisting that there was enough room for us to get out.

The father in Jackie's dream did not realize that he was blocking his daughter. Overbearing parents often don't realize that they are inhibiting their child's development. In the dream, the car is how Jackie moves through her world—her license, as it were. But her father's ploy gets in her way.

In the family system, parents are expected to provide for their children, and the children naturally resent it when a parent decides to keep an inequitable portion of the money for himself. Eleanor resented her father who she felt lived a luxurious existence but who treated her mother and her like paupers. He would dine in expensive restaurants but would take her only to fast food take-outs. She considered him cheap and uncaring.

Although he had a lot of money, Eleanor felt he was simply un-willing to share it with her. He demanded that she get good grades in school, but refused to help pay for her inexpensive parochial school. Instead she was advised to work part-time while in high school to help pay for the tuition. Eleanor became an underachiever at school. By seeking revenge and trying to hurt her miserly father, she sabotaged herself.

Another father had a huge country estate in Massachusetts, but he refused to let his grown-up children use it unless he was there. Since the father spent most of his time in Colorado, the house stood empty for the greater part of each year. Although the father claimed that he worked hard for the sake of his children, his children failed to reap the benefits.

Sometimes parents even reverse the expected roles and count on having their children support them. Bob's mother, for example, encouraged him to become an engineer so he would be able to take care of her in her old age. Many parents, of course, want to be cared for when they are older, but it is not clear that they should be allowed to dictate in precisely what way the money to provide this care should be earned.

Vincent had to make sacrifices to support his parents—all because of an incident between his father and his paternal grand-father, who had borrowed $1,000 from Vincent's father and never repaid it. The father made his children the victims of his resent-ment. He trusted no one with money. He earned many times what his wife did, but he insisted that all their assets be kept separate. He refused to pay for Vincent's college education. He figured that he was entitled to spend the money he earned just as he pleased, regardless of anyone else's needs in the family system. He was also uncomfortable with the use of his assets, constantly complaining about "the damn house, the damn car, the damn yard." Like a miser he seemed truly comfortable only when hoarding his money. The negative effects of this kind of behavior can last for generations.

How the issues surrounding inheritances are handled can become critical problem areas, since it is one of the most com-mon instances in which a parent will appropriate a child's rightful share of money or will deny him any share of their own. Carlos told me that his mother had ridiculed his father because, she claimed, he was a poor financial provider. However, she showed up with $250,000 when the father died. She had withheld the money from Carlos' father's salary and hidden it. The father had assumed he was simply not earning enough, as she was always reminding him. Carlos' mother claimed that the money was rightfully hers, the result of her skillful handling of her husband's money, which he otherwise would have spent. She made no move to provide for her children, nor did she consider that she had any obligation to share this "inheritance" with any other members of the family system.

Some parents do not consider the whole family system when they manage the money of their own aging parents. When Loretta's grandmother, a millionaire, was slowly dying, every one of her five children was waiting eagerly for his or her share of the inheritance. The grandmother had wanted to set up some trust funds for her grandchildren, but the children had manipulated their mother into changing her mind. Just before her grandmother's death, Loretta had a dream in which her mother was looking at some pocket watches belonging to her grandmother who had recently died:

> One had diamonds around it, but the band is macraméd from old string. My mother seems disappointed that Grandma has let these watches get worn out, and she seems upset that she will have to pay for them to be repaired.

Loretta's feeling about her mother's selfishness seems clear. Her mother wanted everything for herself. Her message seemed to be: "Your grandparents belong to me. They are my parents, not yours." But grandparents have a legitimate connection with their grandchildren, and their desire to leave some assets for them reflects a healthy concern for the whole family system.

Leaving inheritances to outsiders or institutions can be an assault on the integrity of the family system. A divorced or widowed man who remarries and then leaves his money to his new spouse without regarding the welfare of his first family can leave his family deprived of their rightful assets. One girl's mother decided that her alma mater needed the money more than her children did, even when the girl had to borrow money for her own schooling.

In other eras, an older sibling would sometimes work and sacrifice his own potential in order to put a younger sibling through college. Or one child, usually the eldest son, would be singled out as the inheritor of money and land. This may not happen so often today, but many children still grow up with the feeling that the family assets have been distributed unfairly. Money, like all other energy coming from parents, must be distributed equitably among all siblings, based fairly on the parents' financial situation.

Overinvesting in one child at the expense of others is unfair. For example, Chuck pursued his studies while his brother entered the family business. But then Chuck's brother decided to strike out on his own, with the complete financial backing of his father. The father gave Chuck's brother an initial loan of $100,000 and later loaned another $50,000 to help out. Chuck's father then died, leaving all of his assets to his wife. Thus one child ended up with $150,000 and the other ended up with a B.A. degree, a situation which caused tension and jealousy.

Unequal treatment of children in a family occurs on a smaller scale as well. Jerry, for example, felt deprived when his parents provided nicer clothes for his sister than for him. She did not have to work her way through college, while he was expected to. In another case, a child of divorced parents got the bad end of a divorce agreement by which the mother was to provide for the son and the father was to provide for the three daughters. The mother became ill and was unable to support her son. The father, keeping to his part of the bargain, did not step in to help, and the son was neglected.

Living in a house which is above or below one's means can be risky. The question to consider is how the whole family will most likely benefit. A teacher once said to me, "The healthy way of living is to buy a house above your means and compensate by buying a car beneath your means." The "Cadillac syndrome"—in which parents spend money on expensive luxury cars or other narcissistically gratifying items while living in substandard housing—is unfair to children. But the opposite behavior can sometimes have exactly the same outcome.

Mike and his wife had a beautiful house in a nice suburb of Chicago, but they refused to maintain it. Among the surrounding well-maintained houses, Mike's house looked like a disaster. He and his wife had thousands of dollars' worth of furniture, Oriental rugs, paintings and accessories, but nothing coordinated or fit together. The house looked like the back room of an antique shop. Mike rationalized that he only planned to live there until his children graduated from high school. This kind of thinking, however, forced his children to live in a messy and embarrassing environment.

Playing Poverty

Parents have their own priorities, and they may think it easier to tell their children that there is no money to spare for what the children want than to explain and justify their money-spending choices. In a maneuver that I call "Playing Poverty," manipulative parents will tell the child that they have no money and expect the child to be fooled. Since children tend to identify with their parents' unconscious minds, the trick does not often work. The child ends up with the confusing sense that his parents are claiming to be poor when they are actually not. The child will grow suspicious if the father earns $150,000 but never buys the child anything, never paints the house, seldom goes out to dinner.

Bernice told me that she and her husband had often complained, in front of their children, about how little money they had. One Saturday when they bought some long-awaited chairs for their kitchen their son said, "Mommy, where are you getting all this money from?" Parents may decide that they need to be frugal at certain times and keep their old beat-up car or put off painting the house. But children may be embarrassed by this behavior and at times may cut through their parents' rationalizations and tell them that they look cheap.

One girl's reclusive father liked to putter around the house during his time off from work, so the family never went away for a vacation. It was difficult for this girl to understand her father's unusual behavior when she compared her situation to that of her friends' families, who often went away.

Some examples of this "Playing Poverty" behavior are much more devastating to children. Hugh's parents said they didn't have enough money to send him to a private camp in the summer, so they made arrangements with a minister and sent him to a religious camp for free—on the condition that Hugh serve as a janitor for the camp. Hugh felt betrayed by this arrangement, especially later after his father's death when it became clear that his parents had had quite a bit of money.

Parents who protest that they are poor may be refusing to assume responsibility for the ways in which they spend their money. Russell's parents continually bought bargain brands, seconds, discount clothes, and cheap toys, even though they had the money to give him nicer things. Some parents will blame their mismanagement of money on their children by making statements like "You are ruining me," or "Do you think I am made of money?" Thomas's father had a different reaction to his children's requests for their allowances or for clothing. He would become red in the face, rip his wallet out of his pocket and throw it at them, exclaiming, "That's all you want—take it."

Money Is Power: Giving with Strings Attached

The democratic family system relies on the equitable distribution of power within the system, and the parent who is unable to share power often finds it tempting to use money as a manipulative device. One patient of mine said of her mother, "With her money, she wielded a powerful sword." A parent must ask himself what he is transferring to his child when he gives the child money or when he buys things for the child. Parents should be aware that when they give money, they are also transferring the fantasy they have about the giving of it. They should use the transfer as a symbol of care and affection. Money should not be used as a manipulative tool to change a child's behavior, to coerce him into conforming to a parent's expectations, or to force the child to be what he is not.

Money can be a motivating factor for a child. It can be part of the positively motivated behavior modification process, such as bonuses and gifts that reward the child's achievements and encourage further accomplishments. The transferred fantasy can be one of trust, for example. One man I know said, "I don't understand why I am so strict with my own children regarding money, as my own father used to give me money and say 'I trust you to spend it wisely. Tell me how much you need.'"

There is also the "exchange transfer": "I'll give you money, gifts, trips, love, if you'll do well in school, behave yourself, and be a success." The child is rewarded if he is living up to his potential; this practice follows from the theory of behavior modification. But the danger is that parents who are out of tune with their child's true potential may motivate him to work for the wrong goals.

The parent who uses money for motivation needs to be extremely careful not to manipulate the child inappropriately. Money talks, and one must be sensitive to what it says so as to avoid the guilt transfer that takes place when a parent's fantasy about giving the child money is "Take it, you ungrateful brat! I could go broke spending my money on you and you wouldn't care!" Many parents feel that so long as they control the purse strings, they control the child. Parents are in a position to buy love or to exact obedience or favors from their chidlren who are financially dependent on them.

Cara's father made it clear that he would not pay for his daughter's education if she pursued a career in acting. He wanted her to be a beautician, which was the last career Cara had in mind. He prided himself on being generous, giving her cars and trips to Europe—but he always chose his gifts in such a way that he could control Cara's actions through them.

Rachel related this story about her father's attempts to manipulate her: "When I was fifteen, I asked my father if he would support me through college. He responded that he would support me only if I would study medicine or nursing or some related field. I refused his offer, since these were not my fields. I wanted to become a writer. He disinherited me.'' He later was sexually abusive toward his daughter.

Once when Thomas was having financial difficulties, his father made repeated offers of room and board if he would move back home. But when Thomas refused the offers, his father did not counter with an offer of financial assistance. In other words, if Thomas consented to eat at his father's table (and stay under his roof and under his domination), then he would support Thomas. Otherwise, the child was on his own. Many parents practice this type of "out of sight, out of mind" parenting, refusing to assume the responsibilities of a parent unless the child stays in the home under their watchful eyes.

President Woodrow Wilson suffered from his father's economic domination. According to the psychological study of Wilson done by Freud and Bullitt, he was kept "in absolute economic dependence" for twenty-nine years and didn't even try to escape his overbearing father's sphere of influence. But his repressed anger came out later on in the form of hostility and attacks on men he saw as father substitutes.

Daniel's mother wielded her fiscal power this way. She did not like her son's wife Mary, because Mary interfered with her own incestuous-style relationship with Daniel. She wrote her son an innocent-sounding letter a few months before Christmas: "I would like you to come home for Christmas, but as you know, the fare is extremely expensive, so I can only afford to pay for one ticket. Love, Mom." Maria's parents also tried to separate her from her spouse. Whenever her parents came to visit, her mother took her out and bought her expensive clothes so that Maria dressed like a princess, and her husband like a pauper. And one young man who had been given an allowance from his parents while he was at college told me that as soon as he began dating a woman his parents did not like, they cut his allowance by more than half.

Some kinds of parenting are calculated to make the child dependent on the powerful father and mother, and money is used as a tool in this effort. Martin's parents continually gave him presents with strings attached. They provided a gift of health insurance so they wouldn't have to pay the bill if he had to go to a psychiatric hospital. They gave him an old car, badly in need of repair. His father expected that Martin would repair it and then (gratefully) permit his father to use it whenever he needed it.

There was a strong element of exploitation in the way Martin's parents treated him. They wanted him to be their slave. He was expected to take care of the family business, an apartment house with about thirty units, and they hired him at a lower rate than they would have had to pay anyone outside the family. They also expected him to be a careful janitor, keeping the place clean, painting the apartments, plowing the snow in winter, and acting as general handyman. They justified this exploitation by saying that Martin's efforts took care of his own future inheritance. Nonetheless, all the properties remained in his father's name.

Abe's father exploited him by agreeing to pay for Abe's therapy, and then failing to pay. He reduced Abe to begging for the money for months, constantly putting him off and acting as if Abe were trying to cheat him. "I can't pay you yet. It's not straight in my mind," he would say. When Abe inquired what his father meant by that, he would not respond. Abe said, "I rationalized that I could contribute most of the money for my analysis myself, but I did not like the fact that there could be no communication about it. My father is clever with money and has made a lot of it. He will not, I think, pass on the knowledge."

To top this off, Abe's father, as executor of Abe's uncle's estate, controlled money that Abe had inherited from his uncle. He used Abe's inheritance to pay the therapist's bills which he had already promised to pay. So the father was "giving" the child money that already belonged to him. Abe's father always claimed that the sacrifices he made for his hard-earned money were for the benefit of his children, but he never put any of their money under their own control.

Other parents keep a rein on their children by lending them money. Parents should be their children's benefactors, not their bankers. If parents want to help a child who needs money, and they have the money, they should give it to the child, not lend it. If they do not have the money, they should try to co-sign a loan for the child. The problem with children being in debt to parents is that it sours the family relationship. Benjamin Franklin once advised people not to lend money to friends, since they will lose both their money and their friends. Children grow to resent parents if they are in the parents' debt. One young man whose father loaned him money said it made him feel terrible; it put a blot on his independence and kept him in thrall to his father. His reaction was a common one. William found it to be true also. After he graduated from college, his parents developed a running account with him. He began to get more and more deeply into debt with them, and this just created a greater masochistic need for him to sink deeper into his depression. His parents constellated this depression by keeping him in debt to them.

Joanne always had "as much money as she asked for," as long as she asked for it. Her mother often told her, "We're giving you money. The least you can do is come and visit us." Clearly the money always had controlling strings. Allocating a certain sum of money per year, a lump sum of money that a parent is prepared to give to the child, is one way to avoid such control. If a parent feels that his child in graduate school will require $5,000 in assistance for that year, and the sum is available, the parent should write out a check for the whole amount and let the child budget himself. There are obviously other alternatives, but to say to the child, "I will send you $200 a month and you can request more if you need it," when you know the child will need $250 a month, is asking the child to beg.

The mishandling of money is most clearly demonstrated when there is not much of it to go around. Cynthia grew up in a poor family. Her parents ran a dress shop which sold seconds and rejects, and her father brought home unfashionable, ill-fitting clothes for the children. Her parents often fought about money, but it was clear who had the powerful upper hand. "There were a couple of occasions," Cynthia remembered, "when the battle became so intense that my father would gather all the cash in the house, his insurance, bonds and bank book and just take off." On one such occasion, the quarrel centered on a winter coat that Cynthia's mother had bought her at a regular store, breaking the father's rule which forbade the purchase of clothes in retail outlets. It took years for Cynthia to come to terms with the fear and insecurity generated by her father's explosion over just this one incident.

Understanding gift-giving is part of knowing how to deal with money. The sentimental view is that one gives gifts out of selflessness and love. In reality, gift-giving is often an occasion to set up the possibility of an exchange—either a fair one or an unfair one. The gift is an exchange of power. The act of giving the wrong gift to a child places him in a difficult situation. He feels he did not really receive a gift; yet he feels that he is expected to be grateful and to give one in return.

Equity and Inequity in Family Resources

A sound family system relies on the equity that is maintained within that system. In earlier societies—agrarian or feudal—children were considered their parents' assets or property, and were to be used as workers for the benefit of the entire family. There were times when a parent owned the right to the child's labor until he was eighteen. Parents had large families in part because they could thus enlarge the potential work force in the household. Also, the more children the parents had, the greater the likelihood that some would survive to support the parents in their old age. At that time, the family structure was not geared toward the equitable distribution of assets and the development of the potential in each individual. When families were larger and risks to life and health were greater, this system ensured that at least a few members of the family would benefit.

In our society, however, with the dominance of the "nuclear" family, the situation has changed considerably. Children can no longer be seen as chattel. The goal of the family system is the development of the growth potential in each individual. To put this notion into practice requires that the family's assets be shared equally among the family members: the king/slave mode should no longer prevail, but should rather be replaced by the king/queen/prince/princess mode, in which every member of the family is equally "royal."

Family assets do not belong solely to the parents. If the family is truly a democratic system, the children have a right to expect a share of the parents' assets, both while the parents are living and after they die. Unfortunately, however, this right is often violated.

Handling and Mishandling Money—The Role Models

Parents give their child role models as well as assets. The responsible parent will not ruin himself financially. But just as important, he will be careful about the style of dealing with money and possessions that he transfers to his children. A child's identification with his parents' unconscious ensures that he will be in touch with his parents' dealings with money.

Parents should try to plan their spending so as to best meet the maturational needs of the whole family. Children have a vested interest in how their parents handle money, since it has a tremendous influence on them both materially and psychologically. For instance, my wife and I felt that it was more important for the family to buy a house than to rent one and thus be able to take more vacations. Our children felt differently; they said they would rather have the vacations. The balance of interests will be different in each family, but the wishes of each member need to be taken into account.

I knew one woman, Edie, who with her husband mastered the art of mere survival. They were what I call the lowest common denominator type—low rent, Salvation Army clothes, but money in the bank. They were content with low overhead. But their system broke down when their son got into Juilliard and they needed to earn more money to pay the high yearly tuition. This forced them to look at their money situation in a new light. While Edie had been saving her limited funds in the bank, her son had been developing his natural musical talents, setting up his own band, working all through high school and earning much of the money for his schooling himself.

Unethical parents may not realize the extent of the influence they can have on their children simply by example. One couple complained to me that their daughter had been caught shoplifting.

It later came out that the parents, who had been robbed of about $10,000 shortly before, had placed a false claim with the insurance company and collected $12,000. The parents expected their daughter to listen to their moral preaching, but didn't realize that she would identify with and imitate their corrupt moral style. Parents cannot expect their children to be honest when they flaunt their clever income tax evasions, switch or remove price tags from merchandise in stores, or tamper with speedometers when they sell their automobiles.

One young man was embarrassed that his stingy father never left adequate tips in restaurants. Another child told me how her mother had swindled the local caterer by having her cater a dinner party for free to "test out" and see if the mother was pleased enough with the service to use the caterer at a larger party she was planning. There was a tacit understanding that if she was satisfied, she would employ the caterer for the larger party. Though the caterer did a fine job, the mother cancelled the order for the large party and felt clever for having gotten the free dinner party from the caterer.

Some parents pass on their inability to discuss money matters. Dick's father would say to him, "It's very impolite ever to talk about money." Dick came to realize that his father failed to understand his child's need to learn about money through the discussion of money matters with his parents. The father didn't want to come to terms with his own wealth and the need for his children to learn to recognize the value of handling their own economic choices wisely. Parents should transfer to their children the ability to use and enjoy money. When Marc's father died and left him $50,000, everyone thought Marc's life would be easy sailing. But the father had hoarded his money and Marc also inherited this destructive money complex which prevented him from making good use of his inheritance.

One father who was manipulative with money provoked his son into a shocking revelation. When the son was twenty and struggling with the question of whether to remain in college or work as a real estate salesman, he had an offer for a job which required that he have a car. He approached his father to ask him to co-sign a loan for $500 from a bank so that he could take the sales position. His father refused, telling him that he should go to work in a factory, as the father was doing. The son was surprised by his own reply: "I don't want to end up like you." The father had unwittingly constellated the realization in his son that the child did not want to follow in his footsteps.

It is important that parents give children a realistic attitude toward money and encourage resourcefulness and creative ingenuity. They ought to use their own assets wisely to enrich the whole family system, sharing the benefits equitably. They should be aware of the messages they transfer when they give money and gifts to their children. Finally, they need to keep in mind that they are their children's primary role models with regard to the earning, saving, and spending of money.

Sexuality and the Incestuous Style of Parenting

The Incest Continuum

The incest taboo, a prohibition of actual sexual relationships between members of the same blood family, is probably as old as civilization. In primitive societies it kept families or clans from being too isolated and exclusive, encouraging a greater variety of cultures. The grown-up child was forced to leave his familiar environment and join some new family. It was recognized at some instinctual level that incestuous relationships could have no positive developmental effect, but would only function to complicate those relationships already existing within the family. This notion is clearly reflected in the Old Testament: "Therefore a man shall leave his mother and father and cling unto his wife, and they shall be one flesh" (Genesis 3:24).

The devastating effects of incest on a child have long been known, but its prevalence is only now being recognized. In *Quadrant* (Fall 1982, p. 15), Beverly Zabriskie noted that one out of every one hundred girls has had some sort of sexual encounter with her father. She quotes one psychoanalyst as saying "There's more of it [incest] going on in good substantial homes than we ever dreamed of," and notes that "in typical incest cases, there is usually a weak, demoralized, or hostile mother, or simply an absent mother, unable to teach, guide, or protect her daughter."

Ruth and Henry Kempe in *Child Abuse* discuss the incest problem in depth. The complicity of both parents is again pointed out: "Many (fathers), gradually sliding toward incestuous behavior, are given the extra push by a wife who arranges situations that allow privacy between father and daughter" (p. 48). This happens when the "parents have reassigned the mother's function to the daughter, in both kitchen and bed" (p. 52). As a consequence, the daughter "is robbed of her developmentally appropriate sexuality," and most "incest victims see themselves as defenseless, worthless, guilty and threatened from all sides, particularly by the father and mother who would be expected to be their protectors" (p. 54).

But it is not only direct physical incest that can have dire repercussions on the psychological well-being of a family. Sons and daughters who are psychologically and emotionally bound too tightly to any family member will have difficulty actualizing their own potential, especially in cultivating relationships outside the family. "Ingrown" attachment—binding instead of bonding—is all too prevalent in the modern family. The ill effects, both for society and for the family itself, of sexual intercourse between parents and children has not generally been disputed. But it must be remembered that incest relates to a much broader range of invasions of sexual privacy and any inappropriate sexual behavior that parents display to and around children.

Erotic, intimate or exhibitionistic display that would be considered inappropriate if acted out in public should also generally not be acted out in front of, or with, a child. In our Western society possibilities for growth occur when a child leaves his family. One major problem with incestuous behavior is that it tends to make children unavailable for other relationships. Psychologically, the children never seem to leave home, so even if they marry they may well not be able to develop satisfying and enduring relationships.

There exists what can be called the incest continuum—a range of behaviors that parents can display to their children, the extremes of which are inappropriate and the balancing point or middle of which is both appropriate and healthy. Parents who are cold toward their children, physically or emotionally, can do as much harm as parents with an incestuous style. To develop self-assurance a daughter needs to feel that her father thinks she is an attractive person in both body and soul. This provides the basis for her confidence as a woman and allows her to realize that she is worthwhile and that, in her future relationships with men, she should be respected. A father who gives his daughter the feeling that she is unattractive is paving the way for the daughter to gravitate toward masochistic relationships. The normal relationship between a father and daughter will always be infused with an element of some sexuality: the daughter is Daddy's little girl, a love object for the father. The father provides her first love relationship with a man, and it is vital that she feel his unconditional acceptance.

One chauvinistic father told his daughter that "any woman can be had." This implied that women cannot be trusted and that they don't have control over their sexual impulses. This woman was sheltered and overprotected, and when she went out with men she was given the third degree by her father, who asked what the man did for a living, where he lived and what his parents did. Then her father would wait up for her to come back and grill her: "What did you do? What did he do to you? How far did you go?" The paradoxical effect of the parent's intrusive questioning, which is incestuous in its style, is often that the daughter will recreate the father's fantasy, fulfilling his prophecy, and wind up becoming involved with manipulative men. The daughter will identify with her father's unconscious and undervalue herself accordingly.

In the extreme incestuous situation, sexual fantasies are acted out. The father fondles his daughter, kisses her in a passionate manner, or makes direct lewd suggestions to her. When the relationship is more subtle, the question is more difficult. A parent's incestuous sexual fantasies can incite premature sexual development, overstimulate the child, and even cause a condition that has been labeled "incest anxiety." The behavior of these parents must be evaluated in terms of the effect that behavior has on the child rather than in terms of the conscious intent of the parents. The question is not whether physical coercion is involved, but whether the child feels uncomfortable with an unhealthy bond to the parent. The popular notion that what feels right is right—"if it feels good, do it"—does not apply here. Even if both parents and child seem to feel pleasure in the over-close bond, the ill effects of that bond will sooner or later become clear. What is "right" should be defined in terms of what is "developmentally right."

Children are dependent on their parents' capacity to be in control of their own sexuality. Fathers and mothers must relate to their daughters and sons as people they love, without treating them as sexual objects. Maintaining a love relationship with a human being while remaining in control of one's sexual fantasies may not always be easy, but certain psychological precautions can be taken. The parent must be careful not to overstimulate the child—for example, by taking "innocent" showers with him or her. What is inherently private must not become public domain within the family. Although I feel that it is healthy for a child to assume that his parents have a sexual relationship, they must not allow the child to listen to the details of their physicality. Discretionary practices, such as locking the doors to bedrooms, are appropriate. Mothers and sons, or fathers and daughters, who sleep in the same bed are playing a dangerous game. Even if no physical contact whatsoever is sustained, the act still constitutes "going to bed with your child," and the unconscious binding it facilitates could be developmentally disastrous and function as an inhibiting factor in the child's psychosexual development.

A seemingly innocent version of invasion of physical privacy comes about in families whose members habitually walk around the house naked. The conscious feeling is "there is nothing for us to hide," but overt exhibitionism within the family is often viewed by the unconscious as advocating incestuous intimacy, which can be confusing to the child. Phyllis told me that when she was very young, her father would stand naked in his bathroom shaving, and he would leave his own door open, not maintaining his privacy. But when she walked by and called out to him, he became very angry with her and sent her away. Her father was paradoxically inviting her presence and then reversing his invitation and rejecting her. Obviously the issue was confused in his own mind as well.

Inappropriate Roles (My Daughter, My Wife)

In some families, the proper relationship between parents and children gets distorted and the children are forced into inappropriate roles. They lose their autonomy and their chance to grow into full, independent adults because their parents overprotect them and sometimes treat them as husbands or wives. The reactions of children to such inappropriate expectations are confusion and at times total submission to or total rejection of the parents.

Parents who are widowed, divorced, single, or in unsatisfactory relationships will often be tempted to become too attached to their children, in order to fill their lonely hours and have their children replace the lost or inattentive spouse. Incestuous bonds can also form when children sense that their parents are not getting along at all, but are only staying together "for the sake of the children." The child senses the vacuum in the parents' relationship and tries to fill it; the function of incestuous longing or behavior on the part of the child is often to bring the parents back together. Through an incestuous association, the child is paradoxically trying to make—or be—a bond between the parents, when the bond that should be there is nonexistent or flawed. One young woman who had wedged herself between her parents had the feeling that "If not for me and my problems, they'd have had nothing between them."

Benjamin, greatly disturbed by his parents' loveless marriage, grew angry and sadistic. He was the type of child who would torture cats, or push children down and claim that it had been an accident. Benjamin's anger had roots in his parents' failed bond. His mother had married a "winner"—the wealthiest man in town. She loved her husband's money, but she couldn't love him. The bonding between Benjamin and his mother became incestuous. In early adolescence he gave her expensive and intimate presents, as though he were her husband, which she did not know whether to accept. Benjamin could not identify smoothly with his father, who tried to compensate for his own feelings of inferiority by dragging Benjamin to athletic events while ignoring other aspects of Benjamin's development. Benjamin grew to hate and disrespect his father, and would curse him to his face, just as he had seen his mother do. His mother reinforced their binding relationship and his father was unable to gain the family's respect.

As her parents' marital difficulties grew greater, Ruth's mother would abdicate responsibility and in effect have Ruth act as wife in her place. "I felt I could not handle him, so I pushed him onto you, and then I became jealous of the attention he gave you," she at last admitted in a letter to her daughter when Ruth was forty-one. This role-swapping is common in incestuous households, when fathers and daughters are thrown together.

The result of such forced intimacy and protectiveness can lead to extreme rebellion on the part of the child, who may have a craving for solitude or a desire to get as far away from the oppressive mother or father as possible. As one frustrated man said about his mother from whom he had at last broken away, "I was sick and tired of being her watchdog." What should have been a natural gradual process of development away from the parents had become instead an abrupt and painful break.

Another abrupt move made by some children in this situation is to get pregnant. Parents who think their teenage daughter's pregnancy is a "mistake" may be failing to understand the underlying reason for it. Some girls get pregnant in order to separate themselves drastically from an unhappy home life. They may see pregnancy and marriage as their only escape from incestuously smothering parents, or they may be searching for a focus in their lives, a possibility for growth that they're not finding in an oppressive home.

Invasion of Sexual Privacy

A child has a definite need to feel that his body is his own. He must feel in control of how, when, and where he displays his body. Parents who encourage their modest daughter of fifteen to wear a bikini are invading the girl's privacy, and she may see her parents' advice as intended to humiliate her.

Suzanne was coerced by her devoutly Catholic mother from the time she began menstruating to undergo a yearly gynecological examination performed by a physician who would then report the results in detail to her parents. Suzanne felt this was intended to prove to them that she was still a virgin. She felt that she had been put through a medical "rape" set up by her mother.

Medical concern is often misused by incestuously motivated parents to invade their child's body. Enemas, issues surrounding contraception, masturbation, inappropriate invasion of a child's privacy during the child's illness, and bath time are all areas of family life that are subject to an abusive parent's incestuous behavior.

A destructive kind of sexual teasing occurs when young daughters have to submit to their fathers' erotic caresses and pinches, or those of other male relatives. Donna's father would attempt to seduce her into willing submission by convincing her that if she was so uptight she would never get a man. Oftentimes, the other parent will participate in the abuse indirectly; Donna's mother defended her husband.

Children may not be forced to submit to actual sexual intercourse with a parent or sibling, but the parents may have incestuous styles which are deeply destructive to their children from a developmental point of view. The parents in these situations commonly have narcissistic needs of their own that were not properly met. Their hunger for attention, love and acceptance from their children then takes inappropriate, incestuous forms.

In situations where invasions of physical privacy are common, children may strongly sense the absence of a mutually fulfilling, satisfying bond between the parents. Often these children will respond to a question about the sexual relationship between their parents by saying "Well, there are two children, so I know they must have done it twice," reflecting the parents' cold and unfeeling relationship.

The Bedroom

Although it is possible that, on some level, the child wants to be sexually stimulated, he is also afraid of that impulse. It has long been accepted that the child is naturally incestuous, but develops an inhibition which is called the incest taboo. When children climb into bed with their parents, they may feel incestuous impulses, but are equally afraid of these desires. Some parents defend their incestuous involvements by saying their child "asked for it." But the child may be only testing, knowing that impulses need to be controlled, and depending on his parents' capacity to control their own sexual impulses. Parents will only reinforce the child's anxiety if they refuse to acknowledge that incest causes the child to suffer.

When a young child has nightmares, he will often ask to climb into bed with his parents to be comforted. A relationship often exists between the contents of the dream and the incestuous longings of the child. One father I knew had a daughter who had nightmares almost every night for three years. She would wake up with a nightmare and climb into her parents' bed to sleep with them. This man had never made the connection that he may have been reinforcing the girl's nightmares, even though he did remember that, as a child, he had also loved getting in bed with his parents. His daughter, in wanting to sleep with her parents, needed their resistance and control, not their complicity in her incestuous longings.

At times, a child's coming between his parents incestuously is covertly or directly related to his fear of being abandoned by his parents. When the child suffers from this fear, it is often because he senses an insecure bond between his mother and father. This sets off a chain of events in the unconscious mind of the child. He must defend himself against this fear, and this often leads to incestuous ploys and plots on his part as he struggles with the incest complex. The nightmare pattern is a common response. One psychotherapist observed that his children began to have nightmares when they unconsciously detected his relationship with his mistress. In a healthy family, on the other hand, the bond between the parents is assumed by the child to be solid.

Having one parent who is strongly or latently homosexual can present a child with an identity crisis. Art's father was a latent homosexual. His mother had an incestuous tie to her brother and only married Art's father reluctantly, her desire for children winning out over her resistance to the match. When Art's parents fought, the father would get into bed with Art, thus accentuating the father's unconscious homosexual tendencies. Another young girl had slept in the same room with her parents until she was fourteen, thereby being a direct observer of her parents' bedroom life and getting the clear idea that her parents had no sexual relationship. This woman later became quite promiscuous and would tell her father (against his will) the details of her affairs. He received an unwanted openness in return for his own lack of privacy.

Inappropriate Comments

Another incestuous style some families display involves frequent conversations or jokes about sex or, especially, the sexual activities of family members. Anything that fosters incestuous fantasies, or incites the possibility of their being acted out, should be avoided. Other parents create the same confusion and embarrassment by telling lewd jokes or teasing their daughters and sons about their sexual maturation. Carolyn's father used to tell her that he thought her breasts were too large. When she lost some weight, he praised her and noted that her breasts looked fine. Her father expected Carolyn to kiss him on the lips. When she got married and began to kiss her father on the cheek instead, he petulantly refused to kiss her at all, and would only shake her hand. He clearly sensed, and resented, that she was no longer ''his.''

With regard to a child's sexual maturation, the wrong parent can sometimes tell the right thing to a child. Is it appropriate for a father to introduce his daughter to the idea of menstruation? Is it appropriate for a mother to introduce her son to the idea of nocturnal emissions and the use of condoms? Subjects with a specific gender identity are best taught by a person of the same gender, just as in other societies when children reach adolescence and have initiation ceremonies, members of the opposite sex are forbidden to participate.

Children need to be encouraged to ask questions about their sexuality and feel comfortable talking about it. Sexual matters can be embarrassing to children, so great care must be taken to insure that the initiation to the topic is not humiliating. Parents often unwittingly embarrass their children. When a girl first gets her period she may feel it is a secret not to be revealed to her father or other family members. When a mother is insensitive to the daughter's needs for privacy, or refuses to discuss the situation, she is in a sense betraying the mother-daughter bond.

Some parents abdicate their responsibility and place the task of sexual education upon a school, a church or a book, or assume that the children will pick up the knowledge from friends. Children need to see their parents as role models, nurturing healthy orientations to their sexuality.

Consequences

Some of the major consequences of incestuous exchanges have been intimated already: the incestuous behavior of parents often distorts the sex lives of their children. It almost always inhibits or prevents the child from developing healthy loving/sexual relationships outside the family.

Some of the effects come to be exhibited in the child's relation to his own body. One girl of eight was forced to take a bath in the kitchen of a vacation house, in full view of the rest of the family. She didn't want to expose herself, but her father insisted. The implicit message was: If you show me your body, I'll love you; if you don't, I won't. Subsequently, this girl developed a great deal of tension and had pains all over her body. A primary symptom was her flatulence—a sign that her body was building its own defenses against the kind of overexposure her father was promoting.

Often when mothers are even covertly incestuous with their sons, the sons will have trouble finding appropriate love objects.

The son may become a homosexual, or a Don Juan, or find that no woman is good enough for him. When the mother has captured her son's libido, or sexual energy, the ability to form satisfying relationships is partially on reserve. Some men whose mothers display an overbearing, interfering, incestuous style seem to lose their sexual drive altogether.

Although prostitutes and promiscuous women may rationalize that the reason they have chosen their way of life is that they were abused by men, they may not consciously realize how their families set them up to get involved with cruel men in the first place. Many of my patients who maintained this lifestyle had experienced an incestuous relationship with their fathers or with another male family member.

A child's sexuality begins with his parents' relationship to their own sexuality and the type of bond they have with each other and with their children. Parents who would like their children to adjust well sexually must realize that they have the power to be an extremely influential role model. They need to observe the incest taboo and satisfy their own sexual needs appropriately. They need to learn to give the child the respect and privacy he needs, and to deal with the subject of sex in a sympathetic and straightforward manner. Positive parents are open to children's sexual questions and explorations, without being intrusive or exploiting them to fill the parents' own narcissistic needs.

Abandonment

Desertion

A child is instinctively so attached to and dependent on his parents that the loss of their presence and support, be it by desertion, financial abandonment, divorce, suicide, or psychological abandonment, can be devastating. The stability provided by a child's parents is vital to the psychological well-being of that child. When the loss is unavoidable, as in death, the child may well unconsciously feel abandoned. In this case he needs an extra measure of support from his remaining relatives.

But many parents find parenting beyond them, and resolve their dilemmas by abandoning the burden of parenting. Some cases are clear cut, such as that of the divorced parent who wants to have nothing to do with his child, or the frustrated parent who cannot come to terms with his existence and commits suicide. Other variations on this theme are more subtle. The affluent often practice institutional abandonment, sending their children to boarding school or leaving them solely in the care of governesses.

Parents who abandon their children may have impressive rationalizations for their actions. In institutional abandonment the parent may believe, at least consciously, that he is giving his child the best opportunities life has to offer—the best that money can buy—but the real intention of the parent is to be free of the burden of child care. Divorced parents who lose interest in their

111

children often defend their abandonment by saying that it is best for the children to grow up in a home free of tension and conflict.

The effect of the absence of a parent will vary from case to case. Sometimes the child will seem to be doing quite well in spite of his loss. Children abandoned by their parents can be shifted, for example, into the hands of a relative such as a grandparent or an aunt. Yet, this move, while often acceptable and even superior to letting the child stay in his original home, does nothing to diminish the fact that in the child's psyche there is no substitute for the true parent. A child suffering feelings of abandonment may have trouble in social relationships with the family, at school, or in the neighborhood. He or she may seem anxious, depressed, or have nervous habits or nightmares. But sometimes the damage is not recognized until it is too late. According to the Kempes, "The parenting may be inadequate because of physical or emotional absence, which early in life results in the failure to thrive syndrome. When the parent is consistently absent in the emotional sense, the child can suffer from a deprivation that may go unrecognized" (*Child Abuse*, p. 12). All too frequently, the parent does not want to become consciously aware of his failed responsibility to his child.

Abandonment often occurs when the parent is dissatisfied with his life and is narcissistically disturbed. Thinking only of their own needs, abandoning parents fail to see how their decisions will affect their children. A parent may be severely frustrated with his employment situation—"I would not be doing this job if I didn't have to support you kids"—which can lead to an irresponsible decision to pack up and leave. Mary Ellen's father acted this out. As soon as his children were in their adolescence, he abandoned his family, bought a houseboat, and sailed away. Mary Ellen saw him occasionally thereafter, but could never feel close to him again. Given such a role model, it was understandable that Mary Ellen found herself involved again and again with irresponsible men such as alcoholics and drifters.

The nomadic parent needs to be footloose and fancy free. He sees responsibility as his enemy. Murray's father, who was a college professor, was a frustrated nomad. Periodically, he would abandon his whole family and disappear for an extended period of time. Murray came to understand his own resistance to getting married and raising a family in terms of his unconscious wish to be a successful nomad. He tried to take his father's irresponsibility a step further by not being tied to a family situation and by not being indebted to or responsible for anyone.

Chip had a lot of energy to direct toward his work, but little energy for any human relationship except that with his mother. He encouraged his own parents to split up; he would send his mother on vacation by herself, and would try to convince her that she was better off without his father. He married young and had two children, but then repeated his parents' inability to establish a mutually satisfying, long-lasting bond. Chip and his wife were soon divorced and Chip would take his children out for the day on weekends. One day when he arrived at the door, he heard one of his daughters say, "Mommy, do I have to go with Daddy?" He then decided he would not see his children at all. He consciously felt that if he could not be their father on his terms, he preferred not to do any fathering at all. This immature decision to abandon his children was an unconscious way of punishing them for rejecting his parental overtures. At first he was not even willing to provide child support. This decision was overruled by the courts, but he maintained his determination not to see his children, avoiding even telephone conversations; when his children were out of his sight, they were also out of mind.

Chip's conscious rationalization was to say that his daughters were being taken care of since all of their physical needs were being met. However, his analysis of his behavior led to the realization that it was a response to their apparent abandonment of him as a father. This reaction to rejection by a child is a sign of unmet narcissistic needs in the parent. Chip was rejecting his child's need to express her feelings about the inconvenience of part-time parenting. The narcissistically disturbed parent may find it difficult to imagine how his children may need him. The child may need to see her father, even though she does not consciously want to see her father at some particular time because of the time and trouble it takes.

Often a parent will find himself in a profession or involved in an interest which makes it difficult for him to fulfill his responsibilities as a mother or father. The traveling salesman, the merchant marine, the soldier of fortune is frequently away from home. This usually places tremendous stress on the parent who is left with the children, and who must play both roles.

June's mother used to complain to her children that their father was always away on business. She felt the need to keep her children close to her, even during their young adult years. While they were in college and graduate school, she expected them to spend all their free time back with the family. If they did not, she took it as a sign that they did not love her. June's mother became an actively devouring parent, but the failure here was June's father's, too, because he abandoned his family to his work.

In the psyche, children have only one father and one mother. Even a stepfather, much as he might be a good parent, can never replace the father. This may help explain some adopted children's obsessive search for their biological parents. This search does not mean that the adoptive parents are doing a poor job. It simply means that the child has an irresistible drive to encounter his "real" parents.

Divorce

Some divorcing parents claim that their children are likely to be better off living with one parent and visiting the other than they would be living with parents who have a destructive relationship. But it is a tragic leap from that notion to a belief that it should be easy for parents to divorce. Parents today frequently feel that their own relationships to each other are completely separate from the fates of their children.

When parents are divorced, the child's instincts about what is right for him may conflict with the parents'. Jose's father virtually abandoned Jose when he was three. His father had himself been abandoned when young. Although Jose still saw his father once a year for a week or two, his father lived two thousand miles away, and Jose's mother, his primary caretaker, became frustrated with her responsibility. When she began seeing another man, Jose's instinct was to go stay with his father, but his mother did not trust the father and would not let him go.

It has been argued that divorced parents have a responsibility to stay in the same geographical area as the child in order to facilitate the child's relationship to both parents. In that sense, Jose's father, by moving so far away, was basically irresponsible in his role as a father. Parenting involves maintaining a long-term commitment to a child. Each individual situation merits careful consideration, but it is the parents' responsibility to do the parenting.

Some divorced parents are experimenting with arranging to live close to one another so that there can be an equal distribution of child-rearing responsibilities without undue confusion and inconvenience to the children. Some even arrange it so that the children live in one house, and the parents take turns living with them. Divorce is, by its very nature, a situation far from ideal, but an effort can be made to even out the parents' responsibilities.

Children of divorced or separated parents are highly sensitive to the precariousness of their position, and feel the threat of expulsion from the family system constantly hanging over their heads. Dawn, who was separated from her husband, was annoyed that her children still enjoyed being with their father. She felt they had turned on her, and she threatened to hand them over to their father. Trapped by her own egocentric need to be the favored parent, she failed to understand that they were simply testing her commitment to them in this unstable situation. Parents ought to tolerate and understand their children's occasional, natural rejection of them without threatening to abandon the children.

The tension in a divorce situation can easily carry over into the parent-child relationship. One boy asked his divorced father if his child support would continue now that he was in college. The father's brusque reply was "I'll have to ask my lawyer about that." But the boy's question was not a legal one, nor was it a demand or a threat; it deserved a simple, open discussion instead of a strained, defensive response. For the father, the whole situation was too emotionally charged to allow for reasonable discussion.

Traditionally, men have been the ones who have abandoned their families. In the event of a divorce, the woman would get custody of the children, and at best, the man would get visitation rights. In recent years, however, some women have been the ones to abandon the family. But no matter which parent chooses an abandoning style, when freedom or liberation is confused with irresponsibility the choice becomes a destructive one.

When there is a divorce, the burden of child care should be equally divided between the parents if at all possible. Children are a joint responsibility, even when a divorce breaks the marriage bond apart. A study of more than 18,000 children from one-parent households done by the National Association of Elementary School Principals and the Kettering Foundation shows that children from such homes have greater disciplinary and health problems, are absent from school more often, and achieve less. Children from these households are also more likely to become the confidantes of the parent with whom they live, and are forced to grow up too soon. They are likely to suffer from anxiety that the remaining parent will abandon them.

I remember hearing about a study in California conducted by a judge who was disturbed by the ease with which divorces were granted. He instituted a mandatory counseling system that couples were required to enter before they could file for a divorce. This proved effective, as a remarkable percentage of the cases resulted in the withdrawal of the request for divorce. Studies such as this show that there are creative alternatives to the finality of divorce.

Suicide

Suicide almost inevitably appears in the child's psyche as an abandonment, and can be very destructive. Children often feel that they are the cause of the parent's death. "If I'd been better," the child thinks, "maybe he wouldn't have killed himself." One man I knew wrote his children constantly, begging them to come take care of him; none of them, for various reasons, did. When he committed suicide, the children felt devastated and permanently guilt-ridden.

In addition to leaving his responsibilities behind, the suicide leaves a legacy of pain and guilt. I have seen instances in which the parent's suicide has apparently influenced the child's decision to have no children of his own, and also damaged the child's ability to handle responsibility in his own life. It also seems that suicides tend to pass along the family curse; they are more apt to have children who also commit suicide. In one instance, the suicide of the grandmother precipitated a nervous breakdown and intense suicidal fantasies in her teenage grandchild.

Psychological Abandonment

Whenever Elizabeth's mother was frustrated, she would tell her daughter, "If I had it to do all over again, I would never have children. I would travel and spend my time on myself." This is an honest confession of the wish to abandon, and it is correctly interpreted by the child as an outright rejection, even when the mother does not desert the child. This same mother acted out her abandonment by forcing Elizabeth to go to summer camp from the time she was five until she had graduated from high school. Summer camp was her mother's way of having the summer off. Other parents will spend much of their time traveling, leaving their children in the hands of babysitters or governesses. One young man remembered that his family's maid always had to sign his report card from school because his parents were never home.

Parents who are so tied up in their work that they have no time for their children are abandoning them, in effect. Parents who are professional students pose even more problems. Not only are they unavailable to their children, their focus being on their studies, but they may well be unable to provide for their families financially, thus exacting from their children a double sacrifice.

When a child needs a parent to help him make a decision, fill out an application form, or pay a bill, some parents will respond with a "hot potato" answer: "Go ask your father," or "I don't want to deal with your problems," or "That's your mother's concern." The parent is trying to pass the buck to the other parent or to another family member. On a practical level, the child does not get the help he requested. On another level, he senses his parents' lack of love and concern for him. Parents who don't want to deal with their children may retreat in any number of ways: drugs, alcohol, sleep, a "do what you like" attitude, the development of debilitating physical or mental illnesses which may be avoidance tactics.

Parents who adhere strictly to a religion such as Orthodox Judaism, which decrees that children who marry outside the faith are to be considered dead or banished, may be paving the way for the abandonment of their own children. Whether the children marry inside or outside the faith, they know that their parents' love for them is only conditional, and that the parents have the backing of the religion—they have God on their side. The parent who rejects his child because of the child's religious preferences or choice of marriage partner may become completely unavailable to his child. If two people are each very committed to their separate religions, perhaps it is a mistake for them to get married. But that is a choice for the people themselves to make, not their parents.

Children can also be abandoned *to* a religion. Thomas's father handed him over to the care of his religious grandfather as soon as Thomas became involved with religion and wanted to go to a seminary. Since Thomas's father was not at all religious, he simply relinquished his parenthood.

Parents will often show how they feel about a child by their sins of omission—forgetting a child's birthday, neglecting to give him gifts, failing to make positive comments about the child, failing to support the child in his exploration and interests. Children who do not feel secure in their parents' love often fantasize that they will be abandoned. Brooke felt this fear quite strongly:

> I remember very clearly being in bed on one occasion with some illness, and my mother going shopping with the words, "I will be back in an hour." The hour was long gone, and my panic rose to terrible proportions—I put a dress over my pajamas and went to the door and screamed for her. Finally I ran down the street barefoot and found her chatting with a neighbor. My relief was unspeakable: I cried a lot and told

her I thought no one was ever coming back. On several occasions after my parents had argued bitterly, my mother said she was leaving and went out of the house (presumably to take a good long walk). I would cling around my father's knees, afraid she had gone forever, and beg him to go and get her back. He always refused, saying she had not really gone. And indeed, she did return. But how is a child to know that? My first real memory of the fear of abandonment occurred at the age of three or so. My father travelled a lot and I wanted to go with him. On one occasion he was to be in the area of his parents' house, so he took me along and left me with them while he did his work. My stay lasted three days or so, and I recall the horror of being left with these old, white-haired people in this cold, dreary house with its funny, musty smells. I cried from the moment he left me until the moment he returned every day, convinced that he would never come back. My poor grandparents never got over that. Neither did I.

Kacey felt that her mother had abandoned her psychologically when she was born, and was never willing to put forth the energy needed to become a truly nurturing, supportive mother. Kacey didn't even feel that she could hate her mother; she felt she didn't have one. As she put it:

On some levels, my mother was a maid. She took care of the essentials of my physical desires or needs. I had a toothbrush and hairbrush, shoes and socks. But anything beyond that, an ear, a presence, a real feeling, even a hurting or struggling person, was just not available. I grew up not even knowing that touching and communicating could be pleasant, that people around me were waiting for me to be friendly with them. Now I fall into the vacuum in my soul by overdoing, overcompensating, being THE MOTHER, the archetype herself in all her opposite ways. It takes an act of conscious will for me to separate myself from this huge swallowing role I play. I had no mother, so I must be that to everyone I meet.

Some children in similar situations will have fantasies about being orphans, or about being adopted children. Liz had such a disastrous relationship with her parents that she wished she *had* been abandoned; psychologically, she had. She told me that she fantasized as a child that she was directly descended from her grandmother, whom she adored, and that her parents had had nothing to do with her birth.

A child of five, in the midst of her parents' divorce, had the following dream which expressed her fear of being neglected or abandoned by her parents:

> I am in a reservoir with my mother and she lets me go, but
> I don't drown. I swim. My father is there too, talking to
> himself on a telephone.

In this dream the girl, who cannot swim in real life, is let down by her mother, who lets her go, and by her father, who pays her no attention and only talks to himself. But in this particular case, there is a happier ending than in some; the girl realizes she can take care of herself.

The secure child is nourished by the confidence that his relationship to his parents and his parents' relationship to each other are strong and enduring. The real meaning of nurturing care, which is the parents' basic responsibility, is the establishment within the child of an inner certainty that the family will survive. This security is based on the parents' investment of time and energy into the relationships, and the child's perception that the parents accept their commitment and responsibility.

Illness and Death

Dealing with Death

Eventually, children will be faced with a death in the family. The death of a parent or sibling will almost always have a devastating effect on a child. Parents cannot prevent such tragedies or their complex repercussions; they can only try to recognize the traumatic effects and work these through with the child in a developmentally sound way. To help their children with their grief, parents must first be capable of dealing with loss themselves; the curse of an ill-processed grief will amost surely be inflicted upon the children.

Parents whose relationships with each other are totally symbiotic are setting up problems for their children. The children may fear that if one dies, the other will soon follow suit. This does in fact happen sometimes. Dana's father died of cancer, and her mother died a few months later of a broken heart. When parents are totally dependent on one another, the children may get the impression that life is completely worthless without an all-encompassing bond, that one's profession and children and friends are comparatively insignificant, and that the death of a loved one is an overwhelming, devastating tragedy from which one can never recover.

When parents fail to heal from the death of their spouses, they bring their child up in a bleak, lonely environment, passing on a

121

distorted view of death, mourning, and love. If people maintain a sense of who they are, independent of their mate, they will not be helpless when they lose their partner, but will be able to work through the loss with friends and family.

A forty-five-year-old woman I know felt for years that she had to call her parents every time she went on vacation, in order to leave a telephone number where she could be reached in the event of their death. Children need to be freed to live their own lives privately. They cannot be expected to plan all of their actions around the possibility of a parent's death unless that death is clearly imminent. In many cases, the subjects of sickness and death are brought up in order to elicit sympathy and attention from children while the parents are actually still healthy. A parent may capitalize on a mild heart problem by threatening to have a heart attack if his child chooses a certain career, or gets married to "that man" or "that woman," or goes on a long trip.

Betty's parents instilled in her the fear that they would die while she was still young, and this fear grew to crippling proportions. After her father did die, she felt that everything precious to her was in danger. She found herself giving money to her boyfriend so that he could pay off his gambling debts. "I couldn't resist," she said, fearing that he was being threatened by gangsters. Betty's phobia became a severe problem to her when she went to nursing school because she was always afraid that her patients were going to die. The fear of death was at the center of her psyche, and this led to an inability to face the fact of mortality, which ironically inhibited her wholehearted entrance into life.

Sometimes children will realize that a particularly egocentric parent is waiting eagerly for a relative to die. Sally was disgusted to realize that all of her grandmother's five children were simply waiting for their inheritance, and that even though her parents were the same age, her mother was openly nagging the father to buy more life insurance so she would be well taken care of and able to travel after he died.

Families should be able to heal after a death, unless, as in Sally's case, the parent is obviously self-centered and seems to have no desire to change. Healing can occur if the family works together, with the parents acting as guides in the grieving process. Children can and should be given extra support and attention at these times. Parents will do well to realize that the family system can be strengthened by the insights gained from facing illness and death honestly. The awareness of death connects people to life, and connects family members to one another. It may take a crisis—an illness, death, or trauma—for a family to be motivated to reevaluate its functioning and move in more life-enhancing directions.

Sickness in the Family

When there is pain in a family, all members experience it. Children may often feel deprived in the difficult circumstance of the sickness of another family member. Because a sick or handicapped person needs a special measure of attention, time, and money from the parents, the other children may feel cheated.

Because of her sister's asthma, Greta's family was forced to live in a chaotic, nomadic fashion. When one child got sick the rest of the family suffered. A great deal of money and security was lost in these transitions, and Greta's parents did not attempt to distribute their energy and time equally among the other family members. Although Greta consciously understood that her sister's health necessitated the moves, she still felt cheated, and resolved never to have children of her own, as they too might become sick.

Jason's whole family system was set up to protect his father. Although his father never spoke about his illnesses, everybody knew their status from Jason's mother: "Don't disturb your father. He's sick again." She even answered for her husband when he was asked a question. Jason was never allowed to relate to his father as an individual. His parents were always too busy, or too sick, to deal with him.

A child's feelings of neglect may seem unfounded, when his immediate emotional and physical needs are actually being met. However, when the focus of concern is obviously directed to one child, the parents must make a conscious effort to affirm the other children, reassuring them that they are equally loved, and encouraging them to help in the support of the family.

Manipulating with Guilt

Sickness and death are difficult enough to deal with in themselves, but they are also quite often used by parents as sources of manipulative control of their children. Some parents manage their children with guilt: "If you don't do what I ask, it will kill me." Parents can play this game by inventing a sickness or exaggerating an existing ailment. It is not uncommon for this kind of parent to develop a heart condition and then use the ailment as a lever to get his own way.

Allan's mother was a master at this type of control. Her intent was to pull him back to her and make him take care of her. The result was that in her presence he felt he had lost himself, as if she had drawn out all of his psychic energy. When Allan did not cater to his mother's every whim, he felt guilty, as if he were being a bad son. "After all I've done for you," she would say. "You'll be sorry when I'm gone." Similarly, Jeff's hypochrondriacal mother, who had suffered from rheumatic fever years before, would periodically say, "You're not going to have me with you much longer, so . . . " He told me his mother had been dying, it seemed to him, since the day she was born. Many fathers will also sing the "death tune"; they will feign a sickness whenever they want love or attention from their busy children.

Sometimes, because of illness, children are asked to become their parents' servants. If a parent has a serious operation the child takes on the role of nurse. Robin's mother had a radical mastectomy, and Robin took complete responsibility for her healing. Under this pressure, Robin self-destructively ignored her own needs.

Other children are forced to take over all the household chores, to take charge of younger brothers and sisters, or to earn money for the family, when a parent becomes ill or dies. Sometimes it is healthy for a young child to serve his parents, but it is unhealthy if that service becomes the major focus of the parent-child relationship.

Traditionally, the last child in the family had the responsibility of taking care of the parents and being a comfort to them in their old age. But parents today should not put themselves in the position of asking their children to do things that may be detrimental. Older people are naturally at times more demanding. There is a strong case, then, for parents to have children while they themselves are still young. Otherwise the younger children will almost automatically have to become caretakers or providers prematurely. When people become parents when they are in their late forties, they run the risk that when their children are themselves in their twenties and ready to separate, the parents might be in need of all kinds of assistance. Parents can plan for their old age when they are still young, so that their children are not burdened with the task of parenting their aging parents. By this kind of planning and foresight parents demonstrate their understanding that young people have lives of their own to lead.

Discipline

Establishing a Disciplinary Style

To discipline a child and set limits on his behavior is an essential aspect of parenting. Every culture places certain demands on its members, and children need to be helped to learn how to meet those demands. Freud wrote:

> The child must learn to control his instincts. It is impossible to give him liberty to carry out all his impulses without restriction. To do so would be a very instructive experiment for child-psychologists; but life would be impossible for the parents and the children themselves would suffer grave damage, which would show itself partly at once and partly in later years. (*New Introductory Lectures*, Vol. 22, p. 149)

The two key elements for a parent to consider in the evaluation of his disciplinary style are effectiveness and fairness. Parents must realize that their disciplinary style is constantly being evaluated by their children. The parent must carefully decide whether the disciplinary act achieves its goal and whether the punishment fits the crime. Children are threatened by parents who overdiscipline them and they rightfully experience such excessive discipline as child abuse. Jeff reported how heartbroken he felt when he was punished unfairly for something his sister had done. He wept, not for his sore rump, but from the anger and pain he felt over his parents' unfairness and the bitterness of being abused by them.

Every family needs to have a disciplinary style—and it should be understood what will happen if any member oversteps the boundaries. What a parent actually does to discipline a child is not nearly so important as what the child *expects* the parent to do. If a child has been brutalized once, even if the parent never touches the child violently again, the child will live under the threat of violence because he expects that it might recur.

It is difficult to decide whether physically coercive disciplinary measures are healthy. A quick slap on the hand of a three-year-old who breaks a lamp can be much more expedient and effective than his parents' attempt to reason with him. As in all parenting situations, the age-appropriateness of any action should be considered. Most parents would set some definite age after which physical punishment is no longer developmentally sound.

There are problems to consider when a parent uses physical discipline. He may create in the child the association of the ideas of problem solving and physical violence. Also the physical discipline may get out of control and become child abuse. However, according to the Kempes, "no punishment is reasonable if it involves the bruising of a small child" (p. 66). They also note that:

> Abusive parents also see physical punishment as an appropriate way to deal with their babies. They may be discouraged when spanking obviously brings no success, but they truly see no alternative and grow depressed by both their own behavior and their babies' responses. Helplessly, they continue in the same vicious circle: punishment, deteriorating relationship, frustration, and further punishment.

Negotiation with the child, various kinds of psychological coercion such as the temporary withdrawal of good feelings toward the child, anger at the child, and the creative use of limited guilt are alternative disciplinary styles. "We are disappointed in you" can be an effective form of discipline when a child has misbehaved, provided the pattern does not become chronic. When a child feels that he consistently fails his parents, he may be left with an inferiority complex.

Disciplining children fairly for their misdeeds and equitably solving arguments and problems arising among family members are difficult tasks for most parents. Many express confusion about what disciplinary methods will be effective without being unduly harsh or unfair. Aside from the injunction against extreme physical or mental cruelty such as beatings, vicious name callings, or threats of physical harm or abandonment, there are no all-purpose rules concerning what constitutes a good disciplinary style; there are only guidelines. The most important guideline is that the parents should ascertain what will work—without abusing the child's body or personality—in a given situation within a particular family. The parent who disciplines ineffectively must evaluate his disciplinary style. To discipline without results is to brutalize one's child. The effectiveness of discipline needs to be measured by the results, not by the intent of the parent. All disciplinary measures should be goal-oriented.

Direct Discipline

A child's refusal to listen or obey will often lead parents to even more extreme actions in an attempt to make that child mind. Threats grow harsh; many parents resort to such statements as "If you don't stop crying, I'll give you something to cry about," which is often the prelude to acts of physical abuse. Parents will use harsh disciplinary measures to stop a child from crying, which may act as a catalyst for more tears.

Other parents are verbally violent. Whenever Ned misbehaved as a child, his father would respond with a crazy threat: "If you do that again, I will cut your hands off." One patient's grandmother used to curse him in Italian: "I should have strangled you, smothered you in your crib. You rotten child, you whore's son, you imbecile. I'll break your neck." Some parents have their children so thoroughly scared of their violent natures and insane tempers that there is actually no need to strike the child. The mere sense of the parental displeasure and disapproval will produce the desired behavior.

A child's manner of enraging a parent often mirrors the parent's own style of punishment. Parents may discipline a child by humiliating him, either in a public display of disapproval such as punishment in front of the child's friends, or in a disciplinary style that is in itself humiliating, such as slapping the child across the face. Ironically, it is these very parents whose children tend to humiliate them in public by throwing temper tantrums and misbehaving when visiting at relatives' or friends' houses.

Malcolm was a messy child, and his mother ineffectively yet incessantly tried to discipline him by constantly badgering him to clean up his room and straighten up his appearance. "She was always on my back," he said. But her efforts were in vain; Malcolm reacted to her discipline by becoming even sloppier. In fact, by screaming at him and nagging him, she set up his resistance and achieved the exact opposite of what she consciously intended. Not only did Malcolm not clean up, but he stopped listening to her.

A few parents are forever grilling their children, trying to catch them in a lie. Kevin's mother used to ask him if he had practiced the piano, and if he hadn't but said that he had, she would reveal that she had stacked the piano books in a certain order and that she could tell they hadn't been touched. She would then start crying, wailing that Kevin must not love her because he had lied to her. In this situation, the parent should be direct: "I see you haven't practiced today." Parents must teach children when and which sort of falsehoods are appropriate (as protective devices against unwarranted intrusion; when happy events are being planned in a surprise for someone close) and when they are not appropriate. They should be especially careful not to transmit a lack of trust, as Kevin's mother did.

More serious problems arise when parents resort exclusively to physical discipline when other solutions are called for. Some parents think a "good beating" is what any child's problem requires. David's father carried this kind of physical response to an extreme: When David's speech therapist told the father that

David had psychological problems related to his stuttering, he replied, "What that kid needs is not psychotherapy, but a rap on the head."

Losing control over one's impulses and resorting to physical violence—slapping a child across the face, pinching, or any other violent attack on the child's physical being—is indicative of a parent's inadequacy. Parents who are not loving or flexible enough to realize that they should try to help the child to understand his wrongdoings and change his behavior, often vent their own anger and frustration on the child who inevitably learns their unhealthy parental style. One girl even internalized this behavior and would slap herself in the face, saying "You are a bad girl" when she was worried about her own behavior. Similarly, violent or extreme punishment for compulsive habits a child cannot control, such as thumb-sucking, or bed-wetting, or masturbation, may also engender masochistic tendencies and low self-esteem.

Indirect Discipline

Discipline is a basic ingredient of adequate parenting. However, some parents discipline their children in such a manner that they can later claim, "I never really disciplined you."

Some parents who always want to be in their children's good graces fear their children will reject them and not love them if they use discipline. Such parents control their children's behavior indirectly. Erich's parents disciplined him through governesses who were given strict instructions about how he was to behave, and how they should handle him if he didn't. His father would simply tell him to listen to whatever his governess said. Some parents will use the other parent as the disciplinarian figure: "Mom doesn't approve" or "Your father wouldn't like that" or "Dad will spank you when he gets home from the office." These are all indirect styles of discipline.

By communicating their real intentions indirectly, parents effectively inhibit the child's ability to be assertive in his own defense. This style of discipline is sometimes acted out in the following manner. When the parents have something negative to

say to their child, they will say it within the child's hearing, but
they will not directly confront the child. The child then consciously feels that his parents did not want him to overhear; he
may feel guilty for eavesdropping. Actually, the parents want him
to hear the criticism; they merely don't want to hear his reaction.

Other parents have trouble following through with discipline.
Val had an example: her father would from time to time explode
irrationally because he had tried to keep all his frustrations and
anger inside. He would then feel very guilty and go off to sit in
a corner. After a while, he would beg Val for forgiveness. She
would refuse, and he would beg her to come over and sit on his
lap. Eventually she would give in and console him for feeling
depressed after having disciplined her.

To discipline effectively, a parent must be able to handle his
own angry feelings and allow his anger to function within the
family system when required. As long as the anger is not irrational,
the child may learn from the parent's expression of it. There is
nothing wrong with presenting a child with a frustrating
challenge, or with disciplining him so long as he knows his suffering has a purpose. As Erik Erikson put it in *Childhood and
Society*:

> Parents must not only have a certain way of guiding by pro-
> hibition and permission; they must also be able to represent
> to the child a deep, an almost somatic conviction that there
> is a meaning to what they are doing. Ultimately, children
> become neurotic not from frustrations, but from the lack or
> loss of societal meaning in these frustrations. (p. 58)

Failure to Discipline a Child

The parent who fails to discipline a child is also creating problems. One woman with five children clearly loved her youngest
best, and protected him fiercely against all assaults, real or imagined. She was constantly going to the child's school to complain
that one of the teachers had treated him unfairly or that another
child had bullied him. As a result, her son grew up to be a
troublemaker. He would do anything he felt like doing, since he

knew that this mother would always back him up and defend him. He had been taught that there was no need for him to accept responsibility for his actions.

A parent who can never say no to a child is doing him a real disservice. At certain stages in their development, children need to work against their parents. Children need a firm base from which to push themselves off and to grow.

Parents who want to discipline their children sometimes do it in a weak, vacillating way. Their children receive an ambivalent response to a definite situation. When the need for discipline arises, parents have to assert their wills; children need controls and guidelines.

Some behavior is appropriate to certain age groups and not to others. One parent discovered some of his pornographic magazines under his nine-year-old daughter's mattress and didn't know what to say to her, though he knew it was important for him to deal with this situation. There are many items in a household that should be restricted from a child. If a parent found that his twelve-year-old had an extra set of car keys, he would not hesitate to take the keys back. This applies to any object or substance which it would not be healthy for a child to have— cigarettes, alcohol, drugs. Children do not have an automatic license to do whatever their parents do; some behavior is for adults only. It is not always hypocritical for parents to have different standards for their children's behavior and their own. The standards should merely be age-appropriate and suited to the situation of each individual in the family.

Parents may find it difficult to agree on the proper disciplinary method for the particular situation. If parents contradict one another too often, the child may grow confused and may begin to play one parent against the other, becoming a wedge in the parents' relationship. Neil and his wife were with their son in a museum, and their son began running all over the place, yelling and behaving wildly. He bumped into an exhibit which Neil caught right before it hit the ground. Neil grabbed the child and told him to stand in the corner of the room and not move until he could calm down. His wife, he observed, not only did not give him any support, but she looked angry at him for disciplining the child in public. Although it is important to try not to embarrass a child, if the child does something in public that needs an immediate response, a parent must intervene. In this case, both parents should have been cooperating in the disciplinary action. In a later instance, Neil told his son to leave the dinner table because of an extremely immature action. His son refused and looked at his mother for support. Neil suggested that his wife take a stance, and she aligned herself with her husband, effectively breaking her habit of favoring the child.

When the parents do not support each other, children can tend to side with, and identify with, one parent. Here, too, this chain of behavior will tend to perpetuate itself until one link is broken. Mathilde's husband beat her until one day she declared she would leave him if he raised a hand against her again. Then he stopped, but their daughter took up his behavior and began to hit Mathilde. For a while, the husband chose not to intervene, and the daughter kept acting out her father's aggression. But as soon as he told her to stop, she did.

When twelve-year-old Kris was caught smoking in the house, his mother was furious, but his father laughed and called it just a sign of adolescent rebellion. The father had inappropriately formed a coalition with his child, siding against the mother and not according her the back-up and support she needed. This kind of parent-child coalition is a sign that the parent is overindulging his child in disciplinary matters. The growing instances of parent abuse in this country indicate that respect for parents, once generally assumed to exist in almost all families, is declining. Within the democratic family system, every member of the family deserves to be treated with respect.

Parents don't always have to agree, of course. In many instances it is appropriate for parents to disagree—and of course it is sometimes inevitable. Differences among members of the family have to be negotiated. It is sometimes even beneficial for a child to get different points of view, to realize that his parents are individuals as well as a team. However, in situations where a distinct problem has arisen, the child needs and deserves to be given more than an ambivalent response.

Jealousy

Families are natural breeding grounds for jealousy. Parents can assist their children in the transition from only child to older child status, but the birth of a sibling will always give rise to some jealousy. There will always be a certain amount of competitive rivalry in a family. It is a natural outgrowth of people living in close proximity. However, jealousy can be created by some parents in families where there is basic unequal treatment of the family members, unfair distribution of the family assets (energy, time, money), and overt favoritism when children sense a parent's focus is on one child to the exclusion of the others.

However, there are times when a jealous reaction is not based on the reality of family favoritism but on the child's need for parental love. This occurs when there is little love in the parent-child relationship. The child may then imagine that the reason he doesn't feel loved is that someone else in the family is receiving all the affection. Actually, the parents may be neglecting all their children.

Attempting to prevent jealousy in a family does not require that parents treat their children exactly alike—especially if there is an age difference between the children. Parents who dress their children in matching sets of clothes when one child is an infant and the other is several years older run the risk of making the older child feel that he is being treated like a baby. Children of different ages will naturally have different bedtimes, privileges and responsibilities within a family, but these decisions should be made with fairness, not just according to the convenience of the parents.

When parents give one child something that should have been joint property, they can create jealousy. Rosemary's parents bought her sister a dog all for her own. The dog bit Rosemary and the bites required stitches on three separate occasions. Her parents did not intervene; they had no sense that their gift to their older daughter was creating an unfair and dangerous situation for their younger child.

Inappropriate disciplinary practices can also create jealousy in a family. One such situation arose when a young boy misbehaved and, as punishment, was not allowed to go to a professional basketball game he'd been eagerly anticipating. To reinforce the punishment, his parents took his sister to the game instead. So she—who wasn't thrilled at the thought of the game—had to bear the brunt of her brother's jealousy. Her parents had set her up to receive the aggression that they had incited in their son.

One thirty-four-year-old woman was told by her mother, "You'd better watch out—your sister's going to catch up with you and pass you." Her parents were encouraging jealousy as though development were a family race, with winner and losers.

Some parents do not even realize when they are playing favorites. Sanford's mother, in the presence of her other children and her husband, said at Sanford's wedding, "This is the happiest day of my life. No, this is the second happiest. The first was the day you were born." Her other children looked at her in disbelief, and one said, "Thanks a lot, Mom."

One girl I know was told by her mother, "When you get married, your husband must come first, not your children. I've always loved your father more than I've loved you." This may have been true, but it was highly inappropriate for her to say it. It created jealousy, and it also gave the girl the feeling that she could be abandoned in favor of her father at any time.

Another father I know told his son, "After me, you come first." But in a democratic family system, *everybody* comes first, everybody's needs must be considered equally. The setting of priorities and the solutions to problems must be negotiated. Often the family will have to compromise when two primary needs come into conflict—but no one member of the family ought to be primary. Equal value should be placed on all family members, and each child should be treated with equal respect and affection.

Problem Solving

There are functional and dysfunctional ways of dealing with the errors and mistakes a child makes. Losing library books, breaking windows, throwing spitballs at school or stones at cars are problems that need to be constructively confronted before they grow into more serious situations.

It is dysfunctional to turn mistakes into catastrophic events, interpreting a mistake as an irreparable tragedy and meting out unnecessarily severe punishment. These parents will inflate the problem, setting up a situation in which the child feels that the problem is insoluble. The positive parent will realize that every problem has a solution. Often, part of the solution is to think of the mistake as an experience from which to learn, rather than as an everlasting tragedy. The positive parent will help the child realize his responsibilities, but will not make the child feel like a hopeless criminal who will land in prison or perish for having made an error. One girl I met was not allowed to go out after school for an entire year because she had disobeyed her parents and came home late from a party one night. She was stunned and confused by the severity of her punishment and suspected that her parents must really dislike her to be so unreasonable.

One common family problem is the seemingly constant fights and arguments that children get into with one another. Some parents try to resolve their children's squabbles by yelling at them; whoever yells loudest wins. Cathy, who had five children, tried this method. When her children screamed, and she became frustrated, she began to scream too, or to hit them indiscriminately rather than trying to find out what the cause of the problem was and negotiating a solution. One of her children was adopted and he seemed to be her favorite. This overt favoritism caused tremendous jealousy within the family. Occasionally, Cathy would compensate for this favoritism by singling out the adopted child for special punishment. Once at a friend's house when her children were fighting, the adopted boy hit his younger sister. Cathy lost control of herself and angrily slapped him in the face. He replied, "You only did that to me because I was adopted."

This may reflect that the child felt he was unfairly treated in other situations as well. Cathy tried to solve these family problems without the beneift of exploration and negotiation. The role of the parent, when there are fights among the children, should be that of arbitrator and negotiator. Parents who throw temper tantrums themselves will only make the problems worse.

Some parental disciplinary styles can transmit to the children the instruction "Be perfect, because mistakes are intolerable." Carol related that whenever she had an accident, such as spilling her milk, she would run and hide in fear. She later found that in her relationships, she was intolerant of anyone's mistakes; she carried on her parents' curse of being unforgiving. This made the development of enduring relationships almost impossible.

Children will often identify with their internalized parents' disciplinary styles. The Kempes write:

> It is distressing to note how often, by the time a child has reached school, he has accepted his parents' punishment as totally valid and rightful. He is usually very much afraid of getting into trouble and may count himself responsible if he does. He has, by then, incorporated into his own conscience and value system the idea that he is in the wrong no matter what he does, and that his punishment is justified. (*Child Abuse*, p. 40)

When the child is afraid to stick up for himself and defend himself against cruel treatment or excessive disciplinary action, he is learning a behavior pattern that will hamper him later in life. In *The Child in the Family*, Maria Montessori notes that "unquestioning obedience . . . leads to the negation of the child's personality, a negation in which the child becomes the object of a justice that is not justice, of injury and punishment that no adult would tolerate" (p. 12).

The child who gives a parent no trouble is often a frightened child. That child doesn't feel safe enough to make a mistake, or even to enjoy himself. There are times when a normal child feels the need to misbehave. The secure child will take a risk, willing to accept the consequences. Obviously, the child who fears excessive disciplinary action will fail to take any of the necessary risks in life, and will grow up timid, unadventurous, and under-developed. One cannot learn to ski if he is too afraid of breaking a leg; one cannot learn to ride a bicycle if he is controlled by the fear of falling. This holds true for most risks in life. I met a thirty-year-old woman who was never able to learn how to drive, simply because of the fear that she might cause an accident. When an adult takes a risk, such as parking his car for three hours at a one-hour parking meter, he is usually aware of the possible conse-quences. What some parents do not realize is that this also holds true for children. They are almost always aware of the conse-quences of their actions, and they should be encouraged to make their own decisions and take the risks they feel necessary. Their healthy development depends on it.

It is now accepted knowledge that children rely on their parents to set limits and boundaries for their behavior. Children expect definite responses to their actions. A disciplinary style should be evaluated in terms of its effectiveness and fairness. In order to discipline fairly, the parent must take the time necessary to ex-plore fully the situation in question. An adequate disciplinary measure permits the child to learn from his mistakes while at the same time setting the necessary limits for his acceptable behavior.

Breaking the Chain

Motivation and Expectation

In an earlier discussion of celebrational parenting, I touched upon the important role the parent plays in motivating his child to pursue meaningful goals in life. Parents have a profound effect on their child's self-confidence, aspirations, and ultimate fulfillment. Parents who know how to motivate their children effectively help them to become flexible, capable, functioning, self-confident adults. These parents are able to celebrate their child's successes and help him deal effectively with situations in which he is not a success.

A positive parent will motivate his child to excel without pushing him too hard or trying to steer him away from what the child feels he is meant to do, and what would lead to a meaningful life. A child's potential should never be limited to matching what the parent has achieved. In fact, a healthy child will often try to succeed specifically in those areas in which his father or mother was not so accomplished.

The parent who knows effectively how to motivate his child will help the child by supporting and praising him, emphasizing—realistically—the child's strong points. At times, this means that the parent will not be able to look at his child with complete objectivity. Although a very subjective experience, parenting needs to stay grounded in reality. The parent who constantly harps on his child's failures will not help motivate that child to succeed. An overly critical parent can produce a hypersensitive or insecure personality.

It should not be the parent's concern how objectively pretty or handsome the child is; children usually have a sense of their own deficiencies and do not need to be reminded of them. Parents should express their positive feelings about their regard for their children, saying, for example, "I like to be with you" and "What you just did was wonderful," showing excitement about the child's experiences. Parents need to give their children a sense of self-confidence so that they can achieve their goals in the world with motivation and confidence. If a child thinks he is unworthy because his parents have always treated him as though he were, he will carry that self-doubt out of the family into his other relationships, and almost certainly fail to achieve his potential. But the other extreme can also be dangerous: the parent who over-praises a child who is average can create frustration and doubt in the child when the child realizes the truth about himself.

Many parents have specific and high expectations of their children, and become very annoyed when the children go off and make their own decisions. The parent who overdirects his child may find that the child becomes rebellious and angry, or may conform externally to parental expectations but lose his own energy, motivation and sense of self in the process.

Another motivational danger is that a parent may try to encourage his child to "be like me." The parent wants his child to follow exactly in his own footsteps as an affirmation of the parent's ego. This maneuver is also tried when the parent unconsciously wants a child to be deficient in the areas in which he himself feels inadequate; this kind of parent cannot bear to have his child surpass him. An adequate parent, on the other hand, can tolerate his child's individuality.

Some parents want their children to choose the same professions they did; many sons and daughters are enjoined to work for the family business, often in positions subordinate to their parents. Children seem to possess a natural instinct to resist this move, but some fall prey to the power of money and allow themselves to be bought out and persuaded into a situation which can lead to a loss of self-image and a comparatively meaningless career. If a businessman's child is an artist, both may grow from the exchange.

Herman's grandfather started a grocery store that his father, Jack, eventually inherited when he was sixty-three. Herman's grandfather lived into his nineties. For the first forty years that Jack worked in the business, he had little power because his own father ruled the business like a tyrant. Jack hated the business even after he inherited it. But instead of wanting more for his children than that, he expected his son Herman to go into the grocery business too and repeat the family curse. He wanted to sacrifice one of his children just the way he had been sacrificed.

In the event that a child does work for his parents, the parent should pay that child a bit more than they would anyone else, because they get a significant benefit in their child's loyalty. To pay one's child the same as one would pay an outsider may be to undercompensate the child for his actual value to the business. Occasionally a manipulative parent will hire a child to do a demeaning job because the parent feels threatened by his child. Larry's father wanted him to isolate himself in Saudi Arabia working on some oil wells. He wanted Larry's help because he knew Larry was a good worker and could be trusted—but he paid him minimal wages because he also unconsciously wanted to keep Larry in a dependent position.

Some parents want their children to suffer as they have suffered. One young woman realized that the reason she had been brought up to be a social misfit, never given appropriate clothes to wear and never encouraged to make friends her own age, was that her mother had always resented her own unpopularity. A patient whose father was a latent homosexual was talking to his father at his wedding. His father said "Didn't I tell you never to get married?" Here the father was trying to pass on his family curse: "I am not happy in marriage, so you won't be either." One parent said to her children when they misbehaved, "I hope when you grow up you'll have children that treat you as *meanly* as you're treating me." This subtle curse may produce in the child a desire never to have children.

Some family patterns are like weeds which move in on the personality and threaten to choke it. Parents must try to control these negative patterns, their family curses, and not transmit them to their children.

The Intrusive Parent

Even parents who do not specifically want their children to be just like them can tend to want to impose their own ideas of what choices are good for children onto their offspring. Children in such families are expected to comply with their parents' wishes fully. Some parents map out their child's career plans—often with crippling results. Sylvia's mother decided on three professions for her three daughters: one was to become a doctor, one was to get married and have children, and one was to become an artist. In this case, the mother was trying to serve as a vocational counselor and determine the destiny of the children, based solely on her own narcissistic fantasies and needs. The children felt as though they had been put in straitjackets; if they veered away from their mother's desires, they feared losing their mother's affection.

Some parents transmit the idea that certain jobs are beneath them and their children. One father didn't respect his daughter's choice to go into banking, since he felt she didn't get her mathematical ability from his side of the family. Another patient was offered a job babysitting when he was thirteen, but his father wouldn't allow him to take the job, saying, "Rich kids who live in mansions don't babysit." On the other hand, parents may prematurely maintain that their children will never rise above a certain level anyhow, so they might as well settle for what they can get. One young woman I know became a secretary on the advice of her parents. It was a job she hated, but she had not been given the confidence necessary to fulfill her true potential.

It is vitally important that a parent respect his child's career decisions. A child's own intuitions and instincts are valuable in this area, and ought to be respected. Violet loved to be onstage, and dreamed of becoming an actress. Her mother misinterpreted this to mean that her daughter wanted a modeling career, so she pushed Violet to enter beauty contests, which Violet hated. Not listening to what her child really wanted, Violet's mother pushed her so hard that she ended up pushing her offstage. The tremendous pressure eventually contributed to Violet's nervous breakdown.

One four-year-old boy drew a cartoon that was a surprisingly exact replica of one he had seen. His mother's reaction when he proudly showed it to her? "A rage of disbelief. She said 'You *couldn't* have done that.'" When he was fourteen, his father said, "You'll never make money as an artist." His parents continued to discourage his artistic endeavors and encourage him to go to architecture school. He obeyed their wishes, but because his talents were elsewhere, he failed.

The positive parent will listen to what his child is really saying when he talks about a career, and then help the child find the energy and resources to pursue that interest.

The intrusive parent will try to dictate the choices a child should make with regard to sex and marriage. Parents may expect their children to remain virgins until they are married; they may want their children to marry for money or status; they may threaten disinheritance if their children marry outside their religion, live with someone out of wedlock, or choose a spouse of whom the parents don't approve. Many parents expect to be provided with grandchildren, and will nag their children incessantly on this issue. The child is being sacrificed for the parents' narcissistic needs.

One young woman told me of the pressure that had been placed on her sister when she was planning to get married:

> She was officially engaged, the wedding planned, a house bought with the down payment as a wedding gift from my parents, but my father couldn't let her go. Her *fiance* was dissected every evening at the dinner table, his every fault examined and magnified, my sister was told that she shouldn't take this and that she shouldn't stand for that. My mother told her she must not allow herself to be alone with him; he might try to jump the gun on the wedding. My sister finally buckled under the pressure and broke the engagement. My father not only blamed her for the money they lost on the house, but told me I had better elope—he'd never go

through *that* again. That was the message repeated many
times in the next four years, but I was supposed to know, according to my mother, that he was "only kidding."

The intrusive parent will try to overmanipulate his child's personality and offer the child a distorted view of reality. One boy's
father told him to be impersonal, manipulative, cold, hard—
"otherwise you'll never get anywhere." His mother added,
"Behave, apply yourself, don't be stubborn—or you won't
amount to anything." This young man felt that he couldn't and
didn't want to be the way they wanted him to be, and yet, by going against their demands, he was worried that he would never
amount to anything.

Even on smaller matters, parental intrusiveness and refusal to
follow a child in his choices can put a painful distance between
parents and children. One twenty-six-year-old woman told me
that she had to keep it a secret that she smoked cigarettes, because
her father "would hit the ceiling." She felt that she would lose
her father's love if she lost his approval because of her decision
to smoke, in the same way she would lose her mother's affection
if she revealed that she was not a vegetarian. These parents
wouldn't let their adult daughter make her own choices.

Adrienne realized how she had come to react against her
parents' many intrusive suggestions. They made her take piano
and ballet lessons when she wanted to play the drums and tap
dance; as a result, she despised piano and ballet and considered
them a burden. They constantly told her to be happy; therefore
she felt she could never express her unhappiness or anger, and
communication ceased. Their implicit message about sex was
"Don't do it—or if you do, don't enjoy it." She became fairly promiscuous. They told her to get a degree; Adrienne took eleven
years to get a degree, dropping out of school five times. They
wanted her to learn only from their experience and she became
self-destructive and rebellious, doing everything and anything her
parents wouldn't like, and later realizing that in doing so she had
neglected her own needs. When a child has a poor relationship
with a parent, even valuable advice is often rejected because the
child must assert himself.

Excessive Expectations

Other parents have such high expectations for their children that they are bound to be disappointed. Some children simply cannot withstand the pressures of excessive parental expectations and crack under the strain. In *Prisoners of Childhood*, Alice Miller writes, "Many people suffer all their lives from this oppressive feeling of guilt, the sense of not having lived up to their parents' expectations. This feeling is stronger than any intellectual insight that it is not a child's task or duty to satisfy his parent's narcissistic needs" (p. 85).

Depression is one reaction to a child's failure to live up to excessively high parental expectations. Anorexia is another classic reaction. "A common feature," says Bruch in *The Golden Cage*, "is that the future patient was not seen or acknowledged as an individual in her own right, but was valued mainly as someone who would make the life and experiences of the parents more satisfying and complete. . . . " Many anorectic girls were expected to be perfect and praised for being perfect. "The common complaint is that they received too many privileges and felt burdened by the task of living up to the obligation of such specialness . . . they turn exceedingly frugal, even self-punishing, because they think they never can repay the debt of their parents' generosity" (pp. 34–37).

While her two older siblings were highly intellectual, Jean was only moderately so. When she got C's in school and would cry, her mother would tell her that she was really a genius. The appropriate thing for her to say would have been, "Do your best. Work hard; the grades don't matter." But she chose a poor motivational strategy; which pushed Jean into a deep depression by fostering an inferiority complex.

One man who had been studying to be a priest decided this career was not for him, and gave up his studies. His father's reaction: "I'm going to die." His mother's: "I guess you didn't have it in you." Instead of supporting their son's revised vocational choice, they could only dwell on their disappointment.

Some parents feel that a child should only choose a career in which he can excel. When Heidi was growing up, she was looked at as the one who could do anything. She was expected to excel in everything she did. When she noted that although she did well in the arts, she found math and science very difficult, her parents refused to accept this. They were adamant in demanding that she succeed in everything. They wanted to consider Heidi perfect. Unconsciously their love for Heidi was conditional; they loved her only if she succeeded in the ways that they had fantasized for her. Heidi's parents thought they were motivating her by saying they knew she would be a top-notch reporter, despite the fact that Heidi had chosen a different career. They didn't support her decision to try to be an artist. She was the victim of her parents' own narcissistic longings; a conflict existed between her parents' dreams for her and her own actual talents. Heidi reacted to these excessive expectations with feelings of self-doubt, worthlessness and self-punishing tendencies.

Brett, too, practiced self-flagellation. She slammed doors on her hands, hit her head against walls, and cut herself with razors. As in many instances of this kind, she was not making a suicidal gesture, but using the mutilation as a penance for her feelings of self-hatred generated by her parents' disappointment in her, and as a reaction against the feeling that her parents controlled her. A child will often do anything to feel independent. Making one's body bleed is a primitive form of expressing ownership. It serves as a symbolic statement: "This is my body. I can feel the pain and see the blood, and I can do with it whatever I choose." As soon as Brett began to have a stronger sense of her own autonomy, she stopped her self-destructive pattern.

Competition

Some narcissistically disturbed parents give their children double-edged messages of motivation, wanting their children to succeed and yet not wanting their children to surpass them.

Most children are instinctively motivated to excel in areas in which one parent is weak. It is common for the child of a successful businessman to go into the arts. At times, the successful, highly competitive parent will inhibit this tendency in his child. He may fail to support his child's interest in the arts by not offering psychological backing or by denying her financial assistance.

Jacob's father seemed to want Jacob to have no personality of his own. Every sign of spontaneity in Jacob's behavior would instantly be squelched. If Jacob became excited about a new activity—chemistry, music, sports—his father would immediately become critical. His father seemed determined not to let Jacob surpass him in any way. He expressed his competitive feeling about his son by never buying him good equipment although he could afford it. Jacob felt that his father would love him only as long as he *didn't* succeed.

A child naturally feels a slight sense of competition with his parents. He wants to achieve more than they achieved. He wants to outgrow them. Healthy parents hope their children will be more successful than they are, or will accomplish more than they did in their lifetime. If parents do not have this attitude, their children may be underachievers.

The Overly Critical Parent

The overly critical parent can quickly destroy his child's motivation. Parents who, in the name of "objectivity," criticize their child's appearance, friends, or aspirations can be cruel and developmentally harmful to their children. These parents don't seem to realize that positive comments can help motivate a child while negative ones may destroy his confidence, his will to succeed, and his capacity to change.

Justin was told by his father that he would never amount to much. This kind of statement can become a self-fulfilling prophecy: children told such a thing can grow up feeling that nothing they do is right. An adolescent told me that if he came home with a C on his report card, he was told "That's not good enough—you can do better." But if he had an A, his father would say, "It must have been an easy course." This boy felt he could never win approval. These children come to realize that their parents have no faith in them.

Overly critical parents will often be ashamed of their children. When one young woman had an abortion, her mother was unsympathetic to her child's trauma and begged her not to tell anyone about it. She failed to realize the psychological complexity of the situation for her daughter. The mother's focus was on what the neighbors would think, not on the daughter's agonizing conflict of having the abortion while wanting the baby. Another young woman who confided to her mother that she was bisexual found that her mother simply refused to believe it.

The role of the family is to prepare a child for life. The ability to function in the world, a critical and competitive marketplace, requires a base of self-confidence and self-acceptance that can only develop out of a parent-child interaction based on unconditional love, support, nurturing, and acceptance. Children without such a base of support will be unable to handle criticism in the outside world, and have a hard time reaching their potential. Parents have a tremendous capacity to motivate their children, to excite them about life's possibilities, and to explore with them the options that are open to them. But they must keep in mind what the child needs to do, and not focus on fulfilling their own narcissistic needs through their children.

Methods of Transformation

Crises Precipitating Change

The breakdowns in family systems often create a need for change. The child usually precipitates change by creating a crisis that exhibits a symptom: he may develop asthma, anorexia, or depression. He may underachieve in school, act out at home by destroying the house, make no friends; he may become chronically angry or anxious or exhibit antisocial behavior. To recognize the need for change, parents must become aware of their children's emotional health.

Often it is the parents who inadvertently fail to allow their child to achieve his potential. By criticizing or providing negative role models, or destructively intervening in their child's life, they create the roots of narcissistic disorders. In these instances, the problems can usually be solved if the parents respond to the symptom as a cry for help. One mother said of her anorectic daughter, "If she were a machine, I'd shake her." This same mother investigated arrangements at funeral homes, in order to be prepared in case her "stubborn" daughter died of starvation. She failed to realize that her daughter's anorexia was a cry for help and a reflection of the breakdown within the family system.

Parents can learn to facilitate change in a family system which is no longer functioning for the child. A child naturally wants to outgrow his parents, and is always seeking avenues of self-fulfillment. This almost inevitably creates a crisis for the parents, since the natural place for the child to develop is in the areas

153

where his parents are weak. When a child is encouraged to succeed in outgrowing his parents, the parents may naturally reexperience their own failures and inadequacies. But this can lead to a deeper sense of fulfillment for the parents, as they can then imagine that they have added something to the world which was not there before.

Many religions are based on the principle of purifying and improving the human race with each successive generation. At the base of these ideas is the principle of the primacy of the child in improving the world of tomorrow.

Changing Parental Behavior

In dealing with crises in the family system parents need to first look at the ways in which they have not been fulfilled, and how they may be narcissistically abusing their children to compensate for their own deficiencies. Then a foundation for problem solving is established. Of course, recognizing a family curse is not the same as eliminating it, and in fact it may be impossible to eliminate it completely in a lifetime. But the goal should be that each generation shows improvement. To break the chain of child abuse, the Kempes suggest that it is vital to help "the parent to relate more comfortably to other adults so that he can develop satisfying relationships and obtain personal support without looking to his children for understanding and comfort" (p. 79).

When a parent starts working on his own narcissistic disturbances, he can see the effects they have had on his children and the family system. Many problems described in these pages can be worked out within the system. Radical problems such as physical abuse or incest must of course be totally eliminated from the system to give children a chance for successful development. But in less serious cases of emotional abuse, parents can learn to modify their behavior so that the chronic nature of the pattern is broken. No parent can transform himself into a miracle worker who solves every problem perfectly, but unhealthy habits can be controlled, either by greater individual awareness or through professional therapeutic help.

The specific effect a given family curse will have on a child cannot be predicted, as demonstrated by the old story of the alcoholic who had two children: one became an alcoholic and the other refused to touch a drop. Each of them, when asked why he had turned out the way he did, replied, "My father was an alcoholic. How else would you expect me to turn out?" Some children repeat the family curse, and some children break free from it. When parents learn to recognize the curses they are passing on to their own children, and try to break them, they offer their children the best chance for a healthy future.

In addition to coming to terms with their own problems, parents can focus on the positive goals of developing the family system so that it promotes positive, supportive, celebrational interactions which help all members of the system. They can look realistically at the line of authority, disciplinary styles, handling of money, and sexual attitudes within the family and make sure they reflect the parents' good intentions.

Growth in the Child

Children who are coming to terms with the emotional abuses they suffered from their parents' behavior can learn to use their negative parents as a springboard for change. They can recognize that they do not want to continue the family curse; that they can transcend their parents' actions and create new patterns for themselves.

Initially, it is likely that children who have been emotionally abused will feel anger toward their parents, or experience depression. But this response will not transform the situation. The legacy of abuse must be worked through, and it can be a painful process. Valerie, aged twenty-five, complained again and again about her mother's mistreatment of her, and how it had damaged her. But since this young woman was now an adult, pointing an accusatory finger at her mother seemed ultimately futile. It was time for Valerie to turn attention to Valerie herself, to see if she could, in maturity, try to break her mother's curse.

A child must first recognize the curse and its effects, and then avoid the old patterns. Just because a pattern has been set up doesn't mean that it has to be followed. "I've always done it that way" is not a valid reason for continuing destructive behavior. Breaking the sequence of unhealthy habits is what counts. One woman had a dream in which someone was biting her leg, and she felt she had to let him do it because she had let him do it before. In the dream, her unconscious was trying to help her understand her masochistic tendencies.

The Role of Therapy

According to Freud:

> Parents who have themselves experienced an analysis and owe much to it, including an insight into the faults of their own upbringing, will treat their children with better understanding and will spare them much of what they themselves were not spared. (*New Introductory Lectures*, Vol. 22, p. 150)

Most therapeutic treatment will involve some analysis of childhood experiences and the relationships with parents. Although it may appear at first that the therapist and the patient are trying to blame the patient's problems on the parents, the therapist is actually trying to push the parents away long enough to deal with the introjected parents—the internalized image of the parent that the child carries around with him, and that sets up certain behavioral patterns in him that he may want to break.

If the child has been abused, damage has been done, and often it cannot be completely undone. The greatest benefit one can expect is that the cycle of destruction can sometimes be broken through greater understanding of the patterns involved. The Kempes believe that "Abusive parents fortunate enough to undergo (psychoanalysis/therapy), can be helped to resolve their ambivalence toward their own parents and to see how their own experiences affect their relationship with their children" (p. 79).

If parents are not happily involved with one another, perhaps they could consider joint therapy. If the problem in the family is primarily with one family member, he or she might embark on a course of psychotherapy. If the problem lies with the family system itself, as evidenced by a crisis in the family and especially by the children's exhibition of symptoms, family therapy may help the family members learn to negotiate—to work with, not against, each other. In any event, only through continued perseverance can the hold of the family curse be broken and children encouraged to lead more productive, fulfilled lives.

Looking to the Future

There is reason to have great faith in people's capacity to change their behavior and to break destructive patterns. The key is the *will* to change, which gives people the capacity to control their actions and to create new patterns of loving responsiveness. The positive growth of individuals within a supportive family system gives meaning to the lives of all of its members and assists them in the fulfillment of their individual destinies. According to John Bowlby,

> The services which mothers and fathers habitually render their children are so taken for granted that their greatness is forgotten. In no other relationship do human beings place themselves so unreservedly and so continuously at the disposal of others. This holds true even of bad parents—a fact far too easily forgotten by their critics, especially critics who have never had the care of children of their own. It must never be forgotten that even a bad parent who neglects her child is nonetheless providing much for him. (*Childcare and the Growth of Love*, p. 78)

We are in a transitional period in the history of the family, one in which parents and children alike realize the importance of meeting their own individual needs, but are still learning how to fulfill the sometimes conflicting needs of individuals within the family system.

The number of single-parent families today reflects the parents' primary concern with their own development and self-fulfillment.

159

Parents are less often opting to stay together in unhappy relationships "for the sake of the children," choosing instead to end marriages that no longer meet their needs. But those parents who stay together because they see their family lives as a vital part of their own destinies are the parents who will provide the optimal environment for the human development of themselves and their children.

The goal of the healthy family community is the maximum personal development of *each* member. Parents can encourage this growth process for their children by trying to replace family curses with flexible, supportive, and celebrational exchanges with their children.

Bibliography

Bowdie, Fawn M., *Thomas Jefferson: An Intimate History*, New York: W. W. Norton and Co., 1974.

Bowlby, John, *Child Care and the Growth of Love*, Middlesex, England: Penguin Books, Ltd., 1965.

Bruch, Hilde, *The Golden Cage: The Enigma of Anorexia*, Cambridge, Massahusetts: Harvard University Press, 1978.

Erikson, Erik H., *Childhood and Society*, 2d rev. ed., New York: W. W. Norton and Co., 1963.

Fordham, Michael, "Individuation in Childhood," in Joseph B. Wheelwright (ed.), *The Reality of the Psyche*, New York: G. P. Putnam and Sons, 1968.

Franklin, Benjamin, *The Works of Benjamin Franklin*, Vol. 2, Jared Sparks (ed.), Boston: Whittmore, Niles and Hall, 1856.

Freud, Sigmùnd, *New Introductory Lectures*, Vol. 22, *Standard Edition of the Complete Psychological Works of Sigmund Freud*, Strachey (ed.), London: Hogarth Press, 1932.

————, and W. C. Bullitt, *Thomas Woodrow Wilson, 28th President of the United States: A Psychological Study*, Boston: Houghton Mifflin, 1967.

Fromm, Erich, *The Art of Loving*, New York: Harper and Brothers Publishers, 1956.

Guggenbühl-Craig, Adolf, *Power in the Helping Professions*, Irving: Spring Publications, Inc., 1979.

162   *Emotional Child Abuse*

Harding, M. Esther, *The Archetypal Images of Father and Mother*, New York: C. G. Jung Fundation, 1963.

Jung, Carl Gustav, *The Collected Works of Carl G. Jung*:
  Vol. 5. *Symbols of Transformation*, Princeton: Princeton University Press, 1954.
  Vol. 6. *Psychological Types*, London: Routledge & Kegan Paul, 1971.
  Vol. 7. *Two Essays on Analytical Psychology*, 2d ed., New York: Bollingen Foundation, 1966.
  Vol. 8. *The Structure and Dynamics of the Psyche*, Princeton: Princeton University Press, 1969. "On Psychical Energy," p. 52.
  Vol. 9. *Researches Into the Phenomenology of the Self*, 2d ed., London: Routledge & Kegan Paul, 1968.
  Vol. 17. *The Development of Personality*, Princeton: Princeton University Press, 1954. "The Gifted Child."

Kempe, Ruth S., and C. Henry, *Child Abuse*, Cambridge, Massachusetts: Harvard University Press, 1978.

May, Rollo, *Love and Will*, New York: W. W. Norton, 1969.

Miller, Alice, *Prisoners of Childhood: The Drama of the Gifted Child and the Search for the True Self*, Ruth Ward (trans.), New York: Bollingen Foundation, 1966. Also published by Basic Books, Inc., New York, 1981.

Montessori, Maria, *The Child in the Family*, New York: The Hearst Corporation, Aron Books, 1970.

Wynne, Edward, article in *Wall Street Journal*, New York, August 23, 1982.

Zabriskie, Beverly, "Incest and Myrrh: Father-Daughter Sex in Therapy," *Quadrant: Journal of the C. G. Jung Foundation for Analytical Psychology*, Fall 1982, p. 15.

Other Titles from Sigo Press

The Unholy Bible *by June Singer*
$32.00 cloth, $14.95 paper

Emotional Child Abuse *by Joel Covitz*
$24.95 cloth, $13.95 paper

Dreams of a Woman *by Shelia Moon*
$27.50 cloth, $12.95 paper

Androgyny *by June Singer*
$24.95 cloth, $13.95 paper

The Dream-The Vision of the Night *by Max Zeller*
$21.95 cloth, $13.95 paper

Sandplay Studies *by Bradway et al.*
$27.50 cloth, $16.95 paper

Symbols Come Alive in the Sand *by Evelyn Dundas*
$12.95 paper

Inner World of Childhood *by Frances G. Wickes*
$27.50 cloth, $14.95 paper

Inner World of Man *by Frances G. Wickes*
$27.50 cloth, $14.95 paper

Inner World of Choice *by Frances G. Wickes*
$27.50 cloth, $14.95 paper

Available from SIGO PRESS, 25 New Chardon Street, #8748A, Boston, Massachusetts, 02114. tel. (617) 526-7064

In England: Element Books, Ltd., Longmead, Shaftesbury, Dorset, SP7 8PL. tel. (0747) 51339, Shaftesbury.